IRIS
An Intimate Portrait

LORRAINE WYLIE

AMBASSADOR INTERNATIONAL
Greenville, South Carolina • Belfast, Northern Ireland

IRIS - AN INTIMATE PORTRAIT
© Copyright 2006 Lorraine Wylie

ISBN 1 84030 176 7

Ambassador Publications
a division of
Ambassador Productions Ltd.
Providence House
Ardenlee Street,
Belfast,
BT6 8QJ
Northern Ireland
www.ambassador-productions.com

Emerald House
427 Wade Hampton Blvd.
Greenville
SC 29609, USA
www.emeraldhouse.com

For Kathy, Jonny, Chris, and Jane.

AUTHOR'S ACKNOWLEDGEMENTS

I would like to thank some of the people who have made this biography possible:

Michael, my husband, who has never doubted my ability; Sam Lowry for his invaluable guidance; the family of the late George Best for their kind cooperation; and, last but not least, Iris Robinson, for her willingness to take part in this project and grant me access to her private life.

LIST OF CONTENTS

INTRODUCTION 7

1 WINDS OF CHANGE 9

2 GENTLE GIANT 13

3 GRIEF AND RESPONSIBILITY 18

4 TEENAGER IN LOVE 23

4 HELLO MRS ROBINSON 28

6 MARRIED LIFE 35

7 MOTHERHOOD 42

8 FULL CIRCLE 48

9 NEW LIFE 54

10 BLESSINGS AND TRIALS 58

11 SACRIFICES 63

12 COURAGEOUS WOMEN 68

13 FAMILY AFFAIRS 73

14   NIGHT OUT 78

15   TROUBLED TIMES 99

16   TAKING A STAND 110

17   POLITICAL LIFE 117

18   NEW SEASONS 124

19   HIGHS AND LOWS 133

20   MAKING A DIFFERENCE 142

21   LIFE GOES ON 149

22   SIMPLY THE BEST 155

23   WHERE TO NOW? 160

     POSTSCRIPT 168

INTRODUCTION

ALTHOUGH NON-POLITICAL, I am able to recognise the sincerity of Iris Robinson's convictions as well as the measure of her success. During her career as a politician she has represented her constituents as local Councillor, MLA, and MP. She has also served as the first female Mayor of Castlereagh Borough Council.

Political opponents may disagree with Iris's opinions, but her constituents appreciate her hard work, dedication, and the lengths to which she will go to help those in need.

This biography was never intended to document an entire life or provide a political platform. It is merely a portrait of the private, political, and spiritual life of a woman who, in a world of shifting values, has remained loyal to her beliefs.

October 2006

Lorraine Wylie

ABOUT THE AUTHOR

Lorraine writes for a variety of Christian and secular publications and is a regular contributor to the magazine LifeTimes. She is employed as a consultant to an international Christian media network based in Northern Ireland. Her husband Michael owns a contemporary art gallery in France, and the couple have three children and a daughter-in-law.

1

WINDS OF CHANGE

LIFE MAY have regained a rhythm of normality but the hardships of war had altered its beat. The world in 1949 was moving at a faster, more exciting pace. The Fifties beckoned with promise and a sense of optimism filled the air. Signs of post-war change were visible in every strata of life.

The previous year, an end to flour rationing had transformed the family menu but when clothing restrictions were lifted, it was fashion's turn for a makeover. With soft, feminine creations, Christian Dior finally swept away the remnants of an austere, utilitarian Britain. Before long the latest trends had captured the imagination of youth, although the cinched waists and full skirts extended more than teenage wardrobes. Suddenly a generation of young people had found a way to express their particular brand of individuality and style. Fashion became synonymous with youth. It may have been the end of a decade, however, it also witnessed an entirely new phenomenon – the era of teenage identity had arrived!

Politically, the Irish landscape was also shifting and changing. By the end of April, springtime had ushered in more than the daffodils. Eire had withdrawn from the Commonwealth and the British government officially recognised the existence of an Irish Republic. At the same time it guaranteed the stability of Northern Ireland's position within the Union for as long as the majority decreed.

A few weeks later, on 25 May, Belfast welcomed Royalty's latest recruits to parenthood. For many, the event was the highlight of the year. People turned out in their thousands to greet the young Princess Elizabeth and her husband, the Duke of Edinburgh. Spectators lined the streets, eager for a glimpse of the happy couple. They were not disappointed. According to popular opinion, motherhood suited the Princess. The future Queen appeared relaxed and absolutely radiant. As for her husband, well, he apparently was even more handsome in the flesh!

During their stay the Royal couple received the Freedom of Belfast City. The press captured the smiles, the cheers, and the celebratory mood of a typical Northern Irish welcome. Eventually the tour came to an end and once again it was time to search for other stories to help sell newspapers. Little did the media realise that Belfast already harboured the seeds of such journalistic scoops.

Nobody guessed the impact that Alex Higgins would have on the world of snooker. At six months, his skills, career, and notoriety had yet to develop and blossom. The hurricane lay dormant as baby Alex dreamed peacefully in his pram. A short bus ride away, in Belfast's Cregagh housing estate, three-year-old George Best was still getting to grips with the intricacies of walking. Like most toddlers, his only goal was to have as few tumbles as possible. Legendary football skills, public acclaim, tangles of love (and even its tragedies) had yet to unfold.

At number 16 Cooneen Way, a few streets from the Best's family home, Mary Collins had her own memories of the decade's highs and lows. Living in such a modern housing development was certainly one of the better events. She and husband Joseph had settled well in the mixed community of young Protestant and Catholic families. Apart from its flat roofs, the estate had a reputation for neat, well-kept gardens and spotless houses. Perhaps the fact that a housing manager made a weekly check on homes, as well as lawns, had a lot to do with their pristine condition!

On 6 September Mary was in no mood for reminiscing. Like most women in the throes of labour, she was more interested in counting contractions and hoping for a moment or two of pain-free respite. Already mum to two young sons, Mary was well prepared for the new arrival. Nurse Sterrit, a woman whose skill and efficiency was appreciated at many home deliveries in the Castlereagh area, had already arrived. Along with the nurse's expertise, Mary Collins was reassured by the presence of her friend and next door neighbour, Mrs Mary Wylie. The latter's softly spoken words and gentle kindliness were always a great source of comfort and encouragement. The friendship and respect shared by the two women was to span over sixty years into the future.

Even today Iris has fond memories of the lady she still calls 'Nanny Wylie'. She smiles at the mention of her name: *"Nanny Wylie is one of those rare people who offer unconditional kindness. She never judges or criticises. Nanny has had a huge input in my life and as a child she was the first person I turned to when things went wrong. She and my mum remain firm friends to this day. My own kids, as well as Peter, love her. There's no doubt that Nanny is a very special lady to the whole family."*

Although the two Mary's continued to address each other as either Mrs Collins or Mrs Wylie, there was nothing stiff or formal about their relationship. The reserved manner of greeting was simply an observation of social niceties that belonged to a generation of another era. Like many friends they found that sorrow is often the glue that bonds the tightest. As a mother, Mary Collins empathised with her friend's grief at the loss of her only baby girl.

Tired and exhausted, Mary Collins finally pushed her first daughter into the world. She had no idea what the future held. Glad that her labour was finally over, she might not have immediately warmed to the news that she was destined to do it another three times! Along with the knowledge of the three children yet to be born, Mary's impending sorrow was also hidden. In just six short years she would experience the searing pain of loss. At the same time, her young daughter would learn some of the skills necessary for her future life in public service.

But, on that day, the young mum was blissfully unaware of the tragedy that lay ahead. With the baby nestled in her arms, Mary was certain of only two things. As well as two healthy sons, she and husband Joseph had been blessed with a beautiful daughter and, when the little lads were introduced to their sister, her name was also clear. In memory of the child her friend had borne but lost, Mary named her daughter Iris.

Iris Collins had arrived.

2

GENTLE GIANT

BY THE time she was five, Iris had made several discoveries. She learned that Jesus loved her, that she was good at reading, and that chickenpox was itchy. She also found that she could run, fast! In later years the latter almost cost her a romance!

As with all children, Iris absorbed the moods and tones of her environment. The impressions merged and created an atmosphere of love and security. Whatever new experience entered her world, its centre never changed – Iris adored her dad. Like most little girls, the story of her parent's romance was always a source of entertainment. She loved to hear how the handsome English soldier had, with nothing but pen, paper, and a stamp, captured the heart of young Mary McCartney. After a whirlwind romance, the two had married and, much to the bride's delight, set up home in Northern Ireland.

By the time his two sons and Iris arrived, Joseph had discovered a hidden talent. A gifted storyteller, his tales of jungle cats and heroic escapades weaved the young family a magical childhood. At Christmastime there may not have been a lot of money, that said, the kids were never short of excitement. After stashing little baubles and trinkets throughout the house, their dad watched with playful glee as his brood searched and found the hidden treasure. When it came to fun, Joseph Collins was an expert!

Although illness contracted during military service in Burma and India prevented him from working much of the time, Joseph did have one job that delighted his young daughter. Iris beams as she recalls the day she boarded a bus on the Ormeau Road only to discover that her dad was the driver: *"I looked round at all the other passengers eager to let them know that their driver was my dad! Boy, was my heart bursting with pride! He winked and gave me a huge grin as I took the seat directly behind him and pressed my nose against the glass partition. It was an incredible moment."*

However, Joseph's bus driving career was short-lived. His health deteriorated and once again it was his wife who shouldered the financial responsibility. With long hours, several cleaning jobs, and a tight budget, Mary kept the family afloat. Her young husband may not have been able to work but his contribution was just as valuable. Despite ill health and unrelenting fatigue, the man that Iris refers to as her 'gentle giant' taught his children patience, kindness, and generosity. When the family's first television arrived, he turned their living room into a mini cinema, transforming an ordinary day into something special. Regardless of what was showing, to the neighbourhood kids, Iris's dad was the undoubted hero.

For five-year-old Iris weekdays were packed with fun and excitement. She loved school and since the first day had managed to attract her teacher's attention. Miss Greatrex noticed that Iris was her only dry-eyed pupil and duly rewarded her bravery. Fifty years later and Iris still remembers the privilege of being chosen to distribute the tiny, rock-hard balls of modelling clay!

Similarly, her primary school teacher has not forgotten the child whose dark eyes sparkled with excitement and fun. Long since retired, Miss Greatrex recalls her little pupil's eager anticipation: *"I have vivid recollections of the day that Iris Collins started her school career in my primary one class. All the children cried except for Iris. Her huge dark eyes watched everything with suppressed excitement. She was eager to get on with things and thoroughly enjoyed each new experience."*

Iris may have enjoyed her introduction to reading, writing, and arithmetic, but it wasn't her academic skills that kept her in the teacher's good books. The youngster's real talent lay outside the classroom. A natural sprinter, her athletic prowess meant that she excelled in the sporting field. In fact, Iris represented her schools at every stage of her academic career.

Whilst Cregagh Primary School did its best to instil the elementary principles of education, it was her parents who assumed responsibility for the family's spiritual welfare. Sunday was a special day and its preparation began on Saturday night. Iris has vivid memories of the family weekend routine when Sunday-best clothes were left out, shoes polished to perfection, and then, one by one, the kids had a bath. The eldest children were sent along to the usual Sunday services and Sunday school, while Iris has the distinct recollection of being first on the 'cradle roll' at St Andrew's Presbyterian Church: *"Like many children, I loved the stories of Jesus and I knew that I was supposed to be a good little girl. I did try for a few days, then I was just as bad as ever!"*

The arrival of baby number six, another boy, meant a lot of excitement as well as noise in the Collins household. Yet Iris, with a child's heightened sensitivity to atmosphere, soon detected an undercurrent of anxiety and sadness. Her mum, busy with the latest addition, was increasingly worried by

Joseph's health. When he was eventually admitted to the Galwally UVF Hospital, Belfast, which then occupied the site of what now is Homebase and Forestside, his young daughter was among the first to visit.

Iris recollects these visits with a poignant mix of sadness and excitement. *"It broke my heart that he looked so ill. Of course, he did his best to hide the pain with a smile and a few light-hearted words."* The hospital itself was also an experience for the child. The beautiful manicured lawns with rabbits running around colourful shrubs and magnificent trees was like a scene from a country estate. *"To a little girl, used to playing in streets, the space was overwhelming! The nurses were also really kind and used to feed me sweets and tried to make the visits as easy as possible for all of us."*

One particular visit stands out in Iris's memory. Although she didn't realise it at the time, it proved an early introduction to disappointment and helplessness. The trip had started out as normal with her baby brother snuggled in his Silver Cross pram and Iris skipping alongside. When they reached a phone box Mary stopped to ring the hospital, anxious lest Joseph was too ill for a visit. All seemed well, so the little family carried on.

At the top of Mount Merrion Avenue, Mary stopped to buy her daughter an ice cream and, to her horror, found that she'd left her purse at the call box. Every penny she owned plus valuable documents were gone. Iris took one look at her mum's face and sprinted back to the red phone box. Never in all her short life had she run so fast. For five-year-old Iris, it seemed the race of her life. It was her chance to help lighten her mum's heavy burden; alas, the phone box was empty. She had lost her race. Disappointed, she cried and turned back to tell her mum the news.

"The memory can still bring tears to my eyes. My mum was absolutely distracted. Somehow I thought I could make everything better for her. There was only one thing I could do

really well and I thought that if I ran my fastest, I would get to her purse before someone took it." Even though she knew it wasn't her fault, Iris still felt a childish responsibility for not being able to help. *"When we reached the hospital, mum's only concern was that dad shouldn't be upset. She hid her own anxiety and refused to add to my dad's burdens. It taught me a little about putting on a brave face. That's something that life requires from all of us at one time or another."*

3

GRIEF AND RESPONSIBILITY

IN 1955 the world mourned the passing of distinguished scientists Albert Einstein and Sir Alexander Fleming, as well as the Hollywood actor James Dean. To young Iris, death was still a word without meaning. However, on 23 June, only three months before her sixth birthday, she encountered personal grief for the first time when her father finally lost his battle for life. The cloak of maturity offers little protection against such deep heartache. But for children, death is surrounded by mystery and fear. Without the tools of comprehension or experience their pain is all the more exposed and raw.

For Iris, the event was compounded by the manner in which she learned of the abrupt end to her childhood. Instead of gentle tones to announce the tragedy, the little girl's loss was shouted from the rooftops. Her voice is filled with sadness at the memory: *"I had been playing round at the local school when some kids came running over. They were screaming my worst nightmare into the air – 'Hey, Iris, your daddy's dead.' Those words rang in my ears over and over again."*

She scrambled up and bolted back home. Running as fast as she could, only this time Iris wasn't looking for a purse, she was searching for hope. *"I knew that dad was ill but he had always been ill. I never for one moment thought he would really die. When I arrived at the house mum opened the door and I could see she was crying. There was no hope. My world shattered."*

The days took on an unreal, confusing quality. Once again Nanny Wylie offered her home as a sanctuary for the bewildered, grief-stricken children. In an attempt to spare them additional sorrow, the older children were excluded from the funeral and spent the afternoon at the cinema. It may have been a decision born out of concern but it denied them the chance to say goodbye and find closure. On the day of his burial, only one of Joseph's children attended, although at three months old his baby son was blissfully unaware of life's tragedy. Mrs Wylie, helpful and compassionate as ever, watched the sad proceedings and rocked the baby to sleep.

Soon Iris was spiralling into a strange and alien world where nothing was safe. The 'gentle giant' had gone. The love and sense of fun he had brought to her life was missing. For the first time she knew fear. Death was no longer merely a word. It had become a reality and Iris was afraid of its power. If her dad could die, so too could her mum. The child was petrified that her mum might vanish from her life. She also learned that grief, at whatever age, is a kaleidoscope of emotion.

Iris attempts to put her feelings into words: *"The effect of my dad's death was immeasurable. I can't begin to express the scars it left. I think it was during that time in my life that the first seeds of insecurity were sown."* As well as the raw, deep pain of sorrow, Iris was angry that her dad had left her. *"If he loved me, how could he go away and leave me? To six-year-old logic, it doesn't make sense. It simply leaves an awful feeling of betrayal."*

The additional problem of local children's taunts and stories of ghosts instilled a terror that her dad might return from the dead. Every time she entered a new year at school Iris could never answer the routine question regarding her father's occupation. *"Admitting he was dead was impossible. I didn't want to speak about it, so I avoided the issue. Right up until I was sixteen, I simply said he was a bus driver."*

To an outsider, the family's future looked bleak. No husband, no money, and six children were a perfect combination for disaster. In an attempt to lighten her load, a local doctor and his wife offered to adopt the baby of the family. Although sympathetic to the childless couple's plight and aware of her own precarious situation, it was a remedy Mary Collins wouldn't accept. She was determined to keep all her children together. Iris was equally determined to keep her mum. *"I became an anxious and stressed child."* She explains: *"I used to lie awake at night and listen to my mum crying into her pillow. She thought no one heard but I did and my tears also flowed. I made a childish but determined vow to do everything possible to help her."*

The combined efforts of widow and child would seem a useless shield against the forces of poverty. But weakness is the perfect opportunity for God to reveal His strength. Although she didn't realise it at the time, God had His eye on her. He had plans for Iris Collins.

The freedom of childhood may have ended but Iris had a new role. As the eldest girl, she became her mother's strongest ally and greatest blessing. While Mary worked several jobs to put food on their table, Iris learned to cook it. She also set about the task of restoring routine and order to her sibling's shattered lives. By the time she was nine, Iris could cook, clean, light the fire, and tuck the younger children into bed.

Brother Ernie still recalls the youngster's determination to keep the family together. Now retired, Ernie has nothing but admiration for his sister. He recounts her input into family life: *"The loss of our father was indescribable. We were so young and unprepared for life without a dad. Even today the pain can be just as fresh. Although she was very young, Iris worked constantly to help our mum. She cooked, cleaned, and shouldered much of the household responsibility. There's no doubt about it, Iris was a fighter and an incredibly hard worker."*

Her family's survival and wellbeing became the nine-year-old's passion. At times, grief seemed too much for her mother. Pain from her loss and worry for her children's future often seemed too much to bear. Although she did her best to hide it from the family, Iris, with her quick intuition, picked up on her mum's despair. However, immaturity and a lack of comprehension made it impossible for the child to grasp the complexities of Mary's sorrows.

It was during these times that her childish fear resurfaced and intensified. She panicked at the prospect of losing yet another parent. Once again it was Nanny Wylie who became both friend and confidant to the frightened child as well as her grieving mum. Iris never forgot Nanny's warmth and encouragement during those difficult days following Joseph's death. *"In her quiet and unassuming way, Nanny brought a measure of calm to all our lives. Nothing ever seemed too much trouble for her. Even though she had her own family, she always made time for us. God certainly brought comfort into our lives through this lovely lady. I really don't know where we would have been without her."*

Regardless of her inner turmoil, Iris was fast developing a reputation as a champion of the underdog. When it came to bullies and her family's welfare, Iris was always ready and willing to fight their battles. Her sister Marlene reflects on how her 'big' sister was fearless when it came to protecting her family: *"It didn't matter how big the bully, if they were bothering any of us, Iris stood her ground. She only had to get wind of a problem and she was there like a shot. People thought she was tough but she wasn't, she was just taking dad's place and looking out for us."*

Iris knew she had a reputation as a tomboy but says it was simply one of her brave faces. *"I suppose I became my brothers' and sister's protector. If I thought they were being unfairly treated or bullied, I was ready to take on the world! I became known for being a bit of a hard nut, yet nothing was further from the truth. I simply wanted to protect my family. It was called survival."*

Iris's childhood was far from easy. Like all children who suffer great emotional pain, the scars went deep and many became permanent. Yet Iris is adamant that she was not totally unhappy. Neither did she resent such an early introduction to responsibility. She is pragmatic about her young experiences: *"I never questioned my role or responsibility. I just accepted it."*

There were, of course, many times of great hurt or fear and events from her childhood can still haunt Iris today. Some scars never heal. *"There may have been the odd time that I resented having so much to do, especially when my friends were out having fun. I simply learned to do things faster. The quicker the chores were finished, the sooner I joined my mates!"*

Her childhood may have had many disadvantages, but it was during her early years that Iris developed a keen sense of responsibility and justice. The family circle was where she practised and sharpened her skills. However, only God knew the role such abilities would play in the future.

4

TEENAGER IN LOVE

THE POST-WAR 'Baby Boomers' were growing up. The new generation was alive, well, and very vocal. With demonstrations and marches, young people expressed their opinions and challenged authority.

For Iris Collins the world had become an exciting place. Mary Quant and Twiggy were the teenage icons of makeup and fashion. With her slim figure and huge dark eyes, Iris revelled in the trendy 'elfin' look. Beatlemania gripped the country and, like most teenagers, Iris was an ardent fan. Every youngster had their favourite individual. For Iris, John Lennon's voice hit all the right notes. Although, it was Paul McCartney's looks that set her pulse racing.

The anxiety of a traumatic childhood still remained. Insecurity was a constant and unwelcome legacy. But life had taught Iris the necessity to adapt and accept. A decade after her father's death, the teenager had developed a mature and pragmatic outlook. Her natural zest for life and an inherited sense of fun ensured a positive attitude. In a house full of noisy siblings, she also found a novel approach to relaxation.

One brother certainly remembers how Iris managed to turn an hour's housework into her own special quality time. He tells the story of how Iris, fastidious about housework, would empty the living room so that she could get on with the vacuuming. *"Of course, we all did as we were told because there was no arguing with our Iris! One day she told us all to sit out on the stairs to let her get to grips with the chores. We sat there for ages listening to the drone of the cleaner."* When it seemed to be going on forever and there was no sign of their sister finishing, one of them eventually peeked round the door. There was Iris, sprawled on the sofa reading a magazine, while the cleaner was propped in the corner!

It wasn't only Iris's brothers and sister who witnessed this mischievous sense of humour. Iris laughs as she recalls how on one occasion she raised the temperature of Cregagh estate by announcing the imminent arrival of Paul McCartney: *"I told everybody that Paul McCartney was coming to Cregagh. Even the cynics believed me. Actually, I was telling the truth. Paul McCartney was coming to visit, although it wasn't the handsome lad from Liverpool they expected. Unfortunately, it was just my cousin whose only link with the young star was his name! Still, it kept everybody guessing!"*

At Knockbreda Intermediate School she was renowned for her athletic ability – Iris entered and won most of the school's sprinting competitions. It was there that Iris discovered her aptitude for speed was not confined to her legs! Teachers soon noticed the teenager's impressive shorthand skills. As well as winning races for school and college, Iris also picked up awards for her ability to write at 200+ words per minute. Little did she realise the future venue for such an invaluable talent.

Iris is the first to admit that her academic achievements ranged within average parameters. However, shorthand was another matter. For Iris, the language of symbolic squiggles proved completely effortless. *"I know I was far from academically gifted! So, for me, Pitman's invention seemed incredible. It just came naturally and I found it easy to attain really high speeds. As a schoolgirl I never imagined I'd be taking notes in Parliament! It just shows how we impose and limit our own goals. However, God has bigger plans for us!"*

By the time she enrolled at Cregagh Technical College other attributes were attracting attention. At just sweet-sixteen Iris was turning heads. One young lad in particular was completely smitten. Huddled against college radiators, Peter Robinson admired his 'dream girl' from a distance. He smiles as he remembers his wistful sighs over unrequited love: *"Iris Collins was definitely my dream girl! To be honest, I just couldn't pluck up the courage to ask her out. I thought I'd never stand a chance. So I told myself she was probably already taken. Yet it didn't stop me looking and hoping! Every chance I got, I'd scan the upper windows for a glimpse of the stunner with brown eyes and short dark hair."*

Little did Peter realise that Iris was just as interested in him. Whilst Peter conjured up an imaginary rival, Iris was indulging in a few political manoeuvres of her own. She chuckles at the thought of the finer points of her romantic strategies: *"For me, it was a case of love at first sight! But he always seemed to be going out with someone else. So I decided to ignore him. Of course, it wasn't long before he noticed that I wasn't noticing him. It's a sure fire way to get their attention!"*

The young couple continued in their respective, though silent admirations. Peter waited until his last day at college before deciding it was a case of now or never. He watched her leave the college grounds and set off in hot pursuit. With a hastily prepared speech echoing in his head, he quickened his pace while trying to appear as nonchalant as possible.

Peter smiles at his marathon along the Cregagh Road: *"I had my speech ready and everything was going according to plan until I rounded the corner on to the Cregagh Road. Iris should have been just ahead of me but, incredibly, the gap between us had widened considerably!"* Unable to understand what was happening, Peter quickened his pace. *"By the time she reached the entrance to the estate, I must have broken the land speed record and was still nowhere near her. I just wasn't fast enough. There was absolutely no sign of her. I couldn't believe it, she'd simply vanished. I didn't know where she lived so there was nothing I could do. How my heart sank as I turned and headed for home."*

What Peter didn't know was that Iris, overcome by shyness at the sight of him, had taken flight and sprinted for home. It's impossible for her to conceal her amusement at the memories: *"I don't know what came over me. I saw Peter behind me and I just panicked. Nerves suddenly got the better of me and I simply took off! I'd been dreaming of that moment for so long but, when it came down to it, I was so tongue-tied and awkward that I decided to run for it!"* Despite the apparent setbacks, it would seem that their lives were destined to be joined.

When Peter learned the identity of his best friend's girl, he employed his budding tactical skills and devised a winning strategy to date her sister. He takes up the story: *"When my friend, Brian, told me that he was dating Iris Collin's sister, Marlene, I couldn't believe my luck! I casually enquired if he ever bumped into Iris and her boyfriend. Once I learned I had no rival, my hopes soared! I asked if he'd mention the possibility of Iris agreeing to a date, although I was fairly certain she'd refuse."* When several days went by without a reply he was sure there was no hope. Then, out of the blue,

Brian called and told him the date was on for Friday night. Peter grins: *"'Great' I said calmly, but nobody was fooled, I was ecstatic!!!"*

Iris's sister Marlene recalls the teenager's excitement at the prospect of a date with the young Peter Robinson. *"She was over the moon! From the very beginning, Iris was besotted with Peter. In fact, believe it or not, half the girls at college fancied him while the other half were after Brian! Yet, apart from me, nobody knew how she felt. Iris was always very good at hiding her feelings."*

When Friday evening finally arrived, a bout of first date nerves had Iris's stomach in knots. As soon as she saw Peter, the love-struck teen couldn't think of a thing to say! She and her sister climbed into the back seat of the Hillman Imp and they all headed for town. *"Peter and I were supposed to go to the cinema so the other two left us in the city centre. However, we'd missed the film so we went to the Wimpy hamburger bar for an ice cream instead. I ordered a Knickerbocker Glory but couldn't manage a bite. I just watched helplessly as the ice cream melted and ran over the glass on to the table. I felt sure this was our first and last date!"*

Peter couldn't miss the melting mess. However, the close proximity and comfortable atmosphere was more than enough to outweigh Iris's lack of appetite. By the end of the evening Peter was convinced that Iris was the girl for him. His certainty was based on that foolproof test of all romantics. With a smile, Peter confirms that *"... after only one kiss, I knew another era in my life was about to begin!"*

5

HELLO MRS ROBINSON

LIKE TALES from the Jules Verne collection of novels, the Sixties began with a trip to the bottom of the sea and ended with a journey to the moon. Jacques Picard and Don Walsh gave science fiction a touch of reality when they broke depth records and descended 10,750 metres below the Pacific Ocean. Later, Neil Armstrong took the first lunar steps and ended the decade in space age style. Political assassinations, a war in Vietnam, and civil unrest throughout the western world marked the intervening years. To add to the drama, nature also contributed a monsoon, volcanic eruptions, and a deadly bout of Hong Kong flu.

At nineteen, Iris Collins didn't need to read about chaos or political instability. It was unfolding on her doorstep. After the 1969 confrontation between police and civil rights demonstrators, violence erupted throughout Northern Ireland.

Like most young couples of their generation, Iris and Peter's relationship evolved against a backdrop of mayhem and civil disturbances.

Although she didn't realise it at the time, the seeds of Iris's political, spiritual, and personal life were sown in this uncertain, troubled era of Northern Ireland's history. Yet, it was in her relationship with Peter Robinson that they eventually flourished and bore fruit. His enthusiasm and intellectual ability for the political arena was infectious. Before long, concern for her country's future as well as a natural sense of justice and compassion ignited the same passion in Iris.

Peter may have sparked Iris's interest in politics but it was his parents who launched her on the journey toward salvation. Both Christians, they had introduced Peter and his sister Pat to the reality of a living God from an early age. They were delighted to share the same message with their young daughter-in-law. Iris remembers Peter's dad as a lovely man with a quiet, down-to-earth nature. She regarded her mum-in-law as both a mighty woman of God and a prayer warrior. Impressed by her testimony, Iris was sometimes a little overawed in her company.

"Peter's mum had such a sense of presence. Sometimes my own insecurities made me feel a little overwhelmed by her indefatigable strength. However, it was this lovely woman who told me of God's amazing love. She taught me about salvation and eternal life. In those early days I used to feel that she had something I lacked. I began to want that same quality of faith."

Apart from church activities, trips to the cinema, and Wimpy burgers, the couple enjoyed a variety of interests. Peter, a keen photographer, processed and developed his pictures in a little darkroom situated in the attic of his parent's home. Their travels while youth hostelling provided an abundance of scenic material. Iris also continued to enjoy her athletic pursuits.

However, it wasn't long before Northern Ireland's rapidly developing political scene became an additional area of interest.

Attracted by common beliefs, Iris and Peter lent their support to the Ulster Protestant Volunteers, a forerunner of the Democratic Unionist Party. Its leader, a local minister by the name of Rev Ian Paisley, was by then taking Ulster politics by storm. Although employed by a city estate agency as an assistant sales manager, Peter found his interest and talent veering more and more toward the current political arena.

Iris accompanied Peter, turning out for whatever protest rallies, demonstrations, or meetings the situation demanded. Even as a teenager, her feet were firmly planted on the ground floor of political life. Almost forty years later, her loyalties and beliefs remain the same. Continuity is the thread that has linked the decades of her political career. Nothing has changed. Except, of course, she no longer wears the mini skirts!

By the end of 1969 Apollo's mission to the moon was old news. But Iris Collins was busy with her own dramatic countdown. After several years of courtship, Peter, with yet another romantic strategy, asked Iris to be his wife. *"I remember the moment perfectly,"* he grins. *"It was by the River Lagan, in my dad's car, that I asked Iris to share the remainder of our lives. I was delighted as well as relieved when she agreed!"* At that time neither Iris nor Peter had any idea of the life that lay ahead. They were about to climb aboard a political rollercoaster that would throw their personal lives into some very frightening situations. Still, as Peter says, there would also be some wonderful moments of triumph and a sense of achievement. It may have been a difficult life that waited, but it was certainly never boring!

For Iris, Peter's proposal was all the more poignant because, at one point, an engagement ring seemed the last thing on his shopping list. When Peter confessed to a few pangs of uncertainty and suggested they part, Iris was devastated. The young man had become central to her life and the thought of being without him was agony. Yet, true to character, Iris hid her feelings well. *"As you can imagine, I felt absolutely dreadful. I can still recall that awful feeling of heart-wrenching sadness. A broken heart is one of the worst pains imaginable. My world seemed to fall apart."*

Regardless of her feelings the love-sick teenager still had to go to work. After leaving college, she had found a job as a secretary to one of the directors at Supermac, Belfast's first out-of-town shopping centre. When she and Peter broke up, Iris would time her walk to work to coincide with his journey into town, always careful never to let him see her! *"I was determined not to contact him, I knew it would be the worst thing I could do. No matter how much I wanted us to be together, I had to be sure it was what Peter wanted too. There was no way I was going to influence him."*

Only those closest to Iris really appreciated the depth of her misery. Her sister Marlene can recall many lonely evenings when Iris sat at home nursing her teenage blues: *"Iris was really upset. Most kids go through similar experiences but for Iris it really was the end of her world. She and Peter were one of those couples who went everywhere together. They were inseparable. When they broke up, my sister was inconsolable. Iris simply put on a brave face and managed to hide it well."*

Marlene confesses that for her trouble has an unwanted but common side effect. Like most women, she finds her solace in food. Iris, on the other hand, completely loses her appetite. *"The weight drops off her,"* Marlene continues. *"It's easy to tell when she's upset or worried, she gets thinner and thinner! She must have lost over a stone when Peter ended the relationship. She'd sit at home every weekend and wouldn't go out. Mum worried about her and wished they'd hurry up and get together again. It was obvious they were meant for each other."*

Iris's silence must have paid off. Peter soon realised that without his 'dream girl' life was meaningless. Fortunately, he knew where to find her. When Iris left work one Friday evening it wasn't long before she spied a familiar sight! *"There he was, sitting on his Vespa scooter, waiting for me! He said he'd missed me and wanted us to get back together again. It took a while for him to convince me that he was certain but I eventually put him out of his misery and agreed to take him back! Then I climbed on board and off we went into the sunset!"*

The couple set their wedding date for 25 June 1970. As the day grew closer, Iris, like many brides of the same era, experienced a few qualms of concern. A frightening bombing campaign, unleashed by the IRA, ripped across the country. Street riots and sporadic outbreaks of violence threatened both lives and property. The impact of such senseless violence ricocheted and spilled into ordinary lives disrupting traffic as well as celebrations and matrimonial lunches. Months of planning were often revised or cancelled altogether. Yet, for Iris, all went well.

Wearing the dress that Peter's mum had made for her, Iris left the house with big brother Ernie. He still recalls the moment when his sister appeared, ready to step into her new role. His voice chokes with emotion, while remembering his sister's big day: *"I'll never forget the picture Iris made as she stood at the top of the stairs. It may sound strange but she was literally shining. She was radiant and truly beautiful. Everyone, neighbours and friends, crowded round to see her. For me, it was a real mixture of emotion. I was so proud to be giving her away. Yet I knew that I was taking our dad's place and it emphasised the fact that he was missing. He would have been really proud to have her on his arm and to see what a lovely woman she turned out to be."*

With her sister Marlene and Peter's sister Pat as bridesmaids, Iris entered through the doors of Saintfield Road Presbyterian Church. Unlike many brides, Iris had no unsettling butterflies to deal with! Her huge dark eyes sparkle as she recalls the day she became Mrs Robinson: *"I have to admit, I wasn't a bit nervous! I knew what I wanted and there were no doubts in my mind. Peter's mum was a wonderful seamstress and my dress, white satin with a cream inlay of lace, was beautiful. It was a lovely day and a wonderful moment in my life."*

Peter sums up his feelings with a smile: *"When Iris and I walked down the aisle together, I was the happiest man alive. It was a really sunny day, in more ways than one!"*

It was during this first walk as man and wife that the couple received one of their most touching gifts. Peter tells about the kindness that can still trigger a few nostalgic moments: *"As a young lad I was an ardent Glentoran fan. At that time my mother worked at the Purdysburn Hospital and we got to know one of the patients, Leo Nellis, quite well. He was a shy, timid man who had spent most of his life in the institution, although, government policy later encouraged him to live within the community."* Leo, also a football fan, was the Glentoran mascot and the friends spent many afternoons listening to the chants of 'LEO, LEO' that echoed all around the Oval.

When Peter and Iris decided to get married, Leo was among the first to receive an invitation. However, he waited until the bride and groom made their way down the aisle before he stood up and offered his gift. Peter continues: *"It was a lovely damask tablecloth that must have cost a fortune. I knew Leo's allowance was small and he must have been saving for weeks."* Peter instinctively knew that Leo's present was more than a celebration of their marriage. *"Leo realised that our paths were about to part. I would be leaving the district with new responsibilities and different interests. His wedding present was also a farewell gift. It meant a lot to me. We still use the tablecloth for special occasions and, every time I see it, it brings back very fond memories."*

On that extra-special day, Iris walked from the church into her new role. However, on the previous evening, Iris was born into a new life. Just hours before her marriage vows, the seeds sown by Peter's mum burst into life. Iris took her place before

God and accepted Christ as her Saviour. She is the first to admit that her journey of faith hasn't always been an easy path. But whatever problems she may have encountered along the way, Iris knows exactly when the journey began.

"On the eve of my wedding, like all brides, I had a lot of last minute things to do but there was something I just had to get right. My future role was changing but my eternal destination had to be decided once and for all. I thought about what Peter's mum had said and, finally, the message of God's love and forgiveness shone through." Alone in the house where she'd spent her childhood, Iris bowed before God and asked Christ into her heart. *"I accepted God's gift of salvation. Although, there were many times in the coming years when my faith waxed and waned, that night before my wedding was the beginning of a truly wonderful relationship with God. Whatever trials life brought, He has never failed me."*

To end the day, they gathered at Drumkeen House Hotel. Ironically, in years to come, the areas where she had played, worked, and celebrated her marriage, would become the site of the offices of Castlereagh Borough Council. It was also where she, as Mrs Robinson, gave her maiden public speech. Called on by her brother Ernie, Iris broke with tradition and addressed her first audience – the friends, family, and guests of her wedding party!

6

MARRIED LIFE

AT ONE time Bangor and Newcastle topped the list for Northern Ireland's favourite honeymoon destinations. However, by 1970, newlyweds wanted something a little more exotic than soggy chips and a stroll along the promenade. The introduction of a flight from Galway to the Aran Islands may have offered an interesting alternative. W B Yeats reckoned the islands 'a haven of literary inspiration'. Although rustic charm, ancient ruins, and the savage beauty of an Irish landscape may get the creative juices flowing, they do little for romance.

When Iris and Peter opted to spend their honeymoon in Majorca, one of the Balearic Islands in the Mediterranean, it seemed they had all the necessary ingredients for a romantic interlude. Iris reminisces: *"Holidays abroad were quite a novel thing at the time. Majorca sounded so far away and exotic! I thoroughly enjoyed the shopping spree for swimsuits and dresses that the Belfast weather would never allow me to wear. Our honeymoon certainly promised to be loads of fun!"*

Majorca turned out to be everything the brochures promised. Peter, however, recalls an aspect of the Mediterranean paradise they didn't expect. *"My goodness, it was hot! We were totally unprepared for the heat. The first day we put on the swimsuits and set off to explore. The exotic sights and sounds were totally different to anything we'd experienced. When we came across a boat trip, we decided it might be fun to spend a few hours soaking up the atmosphere and fishing for lobsters."*

Iris cringes at the memory of their agonising return: *"We hadn't realised just how strong the sun would be. At that time, sun screen wasn't exactly an everyday item for Belfast shoppers! When we got off the boat we were absolutely roasted and must have looked like a couple of gigantic lobsters!"*

The couple hobbled painfully back to their hotel room where, submerged beneath the soothing water of a cold bath, they found an instant remedy for overheated skin. A few hours later their red faces had nothing to do with the sun. Peter explains: *"We hadn't eaten since breakfast so hunger pains were beginning to override the burns! Unable to face the thought of putting clothes on top of our blistered bodies, we ordered from room service while I came up with a plan!"*

Peter reckoned that as the serving staff were mainly female, it was more than likely that a woman would bring the tray to their room. So the couple agreed that Iris would slip into bed and cover her modesty with a sheet while the waitress served their meal. Meanwhile, Peter would hide in the bathroom and wait for the signal that it was safe to come out. But things didn't go quite as he'd expected.

"Iris was supposed to knock twice to let me know it was safe to come out. So I hid in the bathroom, glowing like a Sellafield fish, and listened as the waitress knocked and

entered the room. A few minutes later there was silence. Then, there it was, two distinct knocks." Here was the signal he'd been waiting for and out he came ... wearing nothing but a few blisters! Peter strode across the room, and then stopped dead! *"To my horror, the waitress was standing in the middle of the room, her mouth gaping! The knocks I'd heard was the poor girl bringing in the remainder of our order from the trolley outside. Both of us turned and beat a hasty retreat."*

Iris chuckles at the memory: *"The poor waitress didn't know where to look. Neither did Peter! I just sat there watching the whole spectacle, it was hilarious! Of course, the next morning the other residents didn't know why a group of waitresses fell about laughing when we entered the room. Peter did! Luckily he had sunburn to cover his blushes!"*

Northern Ireland may not have enjoyed the same Mediterranean climate but, politically, temperatures soared. As Iris and Peter nursed their sunburn, Prime Minister James Chichester Clarke struggled with the escalating violence. Scars of civil unrest covered the landscape as cars were set alight and property damaged or destroyed.

The face of politics was also changing. By late summer two newcomers had entered the political arena. The Alliance Party and the Social Democratic and Labour Party (SDLP) offered yet another brand of political remedies. When Ian Paisley won the North Antrim seat at the 1970 Westminster General Election, neither he nor the young Mrs Robinson could have envisaged the future. Over thirty years later, not only would the man they affectionately refer to as 'Doc' still be at Westminster, but both Iris and Peter would join him.

Eventually the young couple returned to the reality of married life. The holiday may have ended but, like all newlyweds, the honeymoon was far from over. The couple arrived burned rather than bronzed with not even enough money for a bus ride home.

The Beatles hit the headlines when they decided that life in a yellow submarine was over-rated and decided to go their separate ways. For many, the break-up of the lads from Liverpool severed the link with the Sixties and youth.

As Iris stepped out of her teens and into her new role as Mrs Robinson, it was to the sounds of a whole new era. By the Seventies groups such as Slade and T-Rex had introduced the musical fantasy of Glam Rock. For the young Robinson's, music was a prominent feature of family life, especially at Christmas and special reunions. There was never any disagreement about the choice of artist or type of music. It was Peter who wrote a variety of songs, including folk and ballads, that he and Iris sang together.

Iris revels in such happy memories of days when the whole family were together. *"There is nothing I love more than a big family get-together especially at Christmas, when private time together is so precious. We both love music and in the early days Peter composed a lot of songs. Not many people know that at one time he sang with his mum in the Christian Endeavour World Convention choir."* Iris admits that her husband's bass voice is actually quite good. Sometimes they sang together or Peter played and she did the vocals. It was a lovely, warm time that's so special to their family.

Iris's love and eager anticipation of such reunions is rooted in childhood. The informality and easy banter is perhaps reminiscent of Christmases spent with her 'gentle giant' when spell-binding stories, delighted squeals, and excited laughter dominated the day. To Iris, a family is more than just a biological origin. As one of life's natural nurturers, she has an inherent need to care and protect, although her early experiences have also sown more than a few insecurities.

Family life is not only about indulging maternal instincts, it is also where Iris finds her own succour. With loved ones around her, she revels in the private roles of wife, mother, sister, and daughter. It is in the domestic arena that Iris finds real fulfilment.

As a Christian, she has found a sense of her individuality and belonging. *"Every woman has various roles throughout life. The people around us have expectations, demands, and wants. Sometimes it's difficult to meet them all. With God, I don't need to be anything other than myself. All pretences are stripped away, He sees me as I am. It is wonderful to know that God knows everything about me and loves me regardless. That, to me, is amazing! In my relationship with Him, I have found true identity. I am a child of God."*

Peter's sister Pat was present at many family gatherings – she had always known her brother's musical ability but she also came to appreciate Iris's more than adequate contribution. Unknown to either Iris or Pat, music would eventually prove a prominent feature in their relationship. However, it would be Pat's future salvation that would inextricably link the two from sisters-in-law to sisters in Christ.

Like many new brides, Iris found that marriage requires a period of adjustment – some time to accept and accommodate individual quirks and idiosyncrasies. After nineteen years of living in the hustle and bustle of a large family, it was difficult to adapt to life as a twosome. *"I soon discovered that marriage wasn't a permanent haze of romantic bliss! It took a little getting used to. For a start, cooking was a bit of a problem. I was used to cooking for large numbers. There were seven of us and normally I had to peel at least fourteen pounds of potatoes at one go. Suddenly, I was preparing just three or four potatoes!"*

Peace and quiet also proved a bit of a problem as Iris adapted to life without the wall to wall sound of noisy siblings. *"Life with a big family is a noisy affair and after a while you don't notice it. However, you do notice the silence. With just Peter and me at home, the house was a whole lot quieter than*

*normal! Looking back, the early days of our marriage did feel
a bit strange, but it didn't take long for me to rub away any
rough edges!"*

But it wasn't just peeling spuds and tranquil evenings that
Iris found strange. She and Peter discovered that their rented
home had an unsettling and disturbing atmosphere. Iris still
experiences the odd shiver at the memory. Even today they
have no doubt as to the exact nature of the problem.

Iris recalls one particularly strange and inexplicable
incident that sent the young couple searching for a new home:
*"We were renting a house at Lenaghan, one of Belfast's quiet,
residential areas. From the moment we moved in, I hated the
place. I really can't explain the atmosphere but it was
definitely eerie. I recall one time when I awoke to the sound of
someone moving around downstairs. At first I just lay there
listening. Then Peter wakened and, like me, he too heard the
noise. We were certain there was an intruder."*

Peter takes up the story: *"I, too, assumed we had a burglar.
I grabbed a stool and went to investigate. To my amazement,
there was no one there! A few days later friends visited and
they also heard noises. Yet, after searching the place, we
discovered nothing. It was only when we were moving that we
found things like Ouija boards in the attic. At some point the
house had been a venue for occult practices. We were happy to
leave!"*

As the couple searched for another house, Iris began to
adjust to the routine of married life. She learned to cook smaller
meals and gradually grew accustomed to the serenity of life as a
twosome. She was also learning about her new relationship
with God. In the infancy of faith, her Bible knowledge was
increasing but still limited. Yet she believed that eternity
depended on salvation.

Slowly, thoughts of her father surfaced and the young
woman began to wonder if her 'gentle giant' had accepted Christ

as his personal Saviour. This question plagued her and Iris often prayed for reassurance. She wanted to know for certain that Joseph Collins was in heaven. God did eventually answer her prayers, but not until Iris was steeped in depression and surrounded by nappies. In fact, just when she needed it most.

7

MOTHERHOOD

ON 5 JANUARY 1973 the residents of Cooneen Way witnessed a strange spectacle. Perched on his brother-in-law's bike, Peter Robinson was receiving a quick lesson in riding a motorcycle. The task was complicated by his instructor's lack of personal knowledge or experience. Yet, as clever sons-in-law know, it is better not to argue with a mother-in-law, especially when she's excited at becoming a granny. Undaunted by Peter's lack of balance, Mary Collins ran along beside him, shouting encouragement. It didn't matter that Peter had never driven such a machine. Mary's chief concern was that her son-in-law reach the maternity ward in time to see their latest arrival, Master Jonathan Robinson!

While Peter weaved precariously through city streets, Iris was suffering the after-effects of a traumatic delivery. Her husband's motorbike proficiency skills were the last thing on her mind. Although delighted with the arrival of her healthy son, the pain of childbirth was unexpectedly severe and protracted. An outbreak of flu had reduced maternity staff to a minimum and she had been left alone for long periods during labour. By the time Jonathan was born, his mum had suffered third degree tears and a phobic fear of pregnancy. In fact, it was six years before Iris would or could consider another baby. Unfortunately for Iris, she was not one of those women who simply blossom with prospective motherhood. On the contrary, for her, pregnancy meant nine months of continual sickness, intravenous drips, and doses of stout and egg drinks!

"When I found out that Jonathan was on the way, I rushed to a phone box bursting to tell Peter the news. He was absolutely delighted at the prospect of being a dad! I was completely unprepared for the constant nausea and sickness." The bouts of sickness, usually worse in the morning, made the journey to work a nightmare. Iris recalls how on one occasion she had to get off the bus and make a dash for the nearest alleyway. *"It was awful. A lady came out, thought I was drunk, called me some questionable names and sent me on my way. I hadn't even the strength to answer back!"*

Now a family, the couple were delighted to learn that they had been offered a flat in the Sunderland Road area of Castlereagh. It was during their first visit that Iris met her new neighbour and lifelong friend, Hazel Pickervance. She reflects on her first meeting with the excited couple: *"Iris and Peter came up to have a look round but they had no key. The dimensions were similar to our place so I invited them in to see our rooms."*

The young women soon found they had a lot in common, while Peter, an obvious Glentoran fan, was always up for a bit of good-natured banter. Hazel and Iris spent many afternoons wheeling their prams down the Cregagh Road and browsing round shops. Hazel could never have guessed the direction her friend's life would take. *"Iris and I shared many laughs and, regardless of what the years have brought or how circumstances have changed, she's still the same down-to-earth girl I've always known."*

Life should have been good. She was married to her teenage sweetheart, had a lovely baby, a good neighbour who was also a friend, and she lived close to her family. But the early days of motherhood were far from happy. Actually, for Iris, life had never seemed so bleak. Suddenly a sense of hopelessness and apathy began to cloud her naturally sunny outlook. Before long, the young mum could find neither the incentive nor strength to do even the most menial tasks. Days merged into night as she lost interest in all that went on around her.

Confused and bewildered by such unfamiliar feelings, Iris had no idea she was suffering from the distressing but common condition, clinically known as Postnatal Depression. Well-meaning advice to cheer up and appreciate life's blessings only made her feel even more inadequate. Any woman who has suffered the condition will understand the awful sense of hopelessness it can cause. What should be one of life's most special events is robbed of joy and appreciation.

The recollection of that time is vividly etched on her mind. *"At one point, even getting dressed became too much hassle and I'd sit around in my dressing gown wallowing in a sense of complete inadequacy."* The fact that other women seemed to cope with motherhood five or six times over underscored her sense of failure. Modern medicine may be quick to recognise the symptoms; however, for women of Iris's generation, the remedy was more often a stern lecture from well-meaning friends or relatives. As Iris discovered, physical and emotional support went a long way toward her recovery. *"My sister was a great help as she often took Jonathan to let me sleep and Peter did his best to keep things as normal as possible. It wasn't an easy time but I did eventually come out the other side."*

Depression, in any form, affects more than the individual concerned. It often splashes and spills into the lives of those closest to them. While Iris suffered the distressing symptoms of hormonal chaos, it was Peter who struggled to maintain a sense of normality and routine. Already his Party's General Secretary, the young father was busy trying to juggle the demands of a new career as well as family life.

Two years previously, Peter had suffered his own emotional upheaval when his best friend, Harry Beggs, was murdered by an IRA bomb explosion at the offices of the Northern Ireland Electricity Service. The anger and bitterness that stemmed from his grief played a major part in Peter's motivation toward a career in politics. He sighs at the painful memories: *"Harry was my best friend at school. We played football together and shared many hopes and dreams. He went to work for the Electricity Service while I chose a career in estate agency. I met and married Iris but Harry never got to experience more than twenty-three years of life. Terrorists cut it short and launched him into eternity."* Peter goes on to tell how the tragic event ignited a strong desire for peace in his country. *"I wanted to play my role in bringing that about and the political route seemed the right way to go."*

The birth of baby Jonathan added a few domestic upheavals and things at home became particularly difficult. Like many husbands Peter was confused by his wife's sudden change in personality. *"I didn't understand what was happening to Iris. The happy, bubbly personality I knew had gone. She was so depressed and deeply unhappy; I didn't know what to do for her. It was also a busy time in Northern Ireland's history but there was only one choice, my family came first. Iris and the baby needed my support and presence at home."*

After a while a definite diagnosis provided the couple with the information that enabled them to cope with the situation. With the realisation that the condition wasn't permanent, things gradually became easier. Peter continues: *"By finding the right treatment and giving Iris the support she needed, life began to improve. Being at home and looking after the baby meant I got to spend more time with our son, that was the good part. Today, the need for fathers to be with their family, especially in the early days following birth is well recognised. Then there was no such thing as paternity leave."*

According to one Christian doctor who runs a busy practice in Belfast's inner city, Postnatal Depression, or 'baby blues', is a fairly common condition. She explains how many new mums can feel a sense of failure: *"Baby blues usually lasts a few days or weeks following a birth. It normally disappears without treatment. In some cases a bout of deeper depression can follow. Mums feel inadequate and blame themselves for not being the perfect mother. As with everything in life, Christians are not exempt! They often query the quality of their faith."*

Peter's presence may have provided Iris with much-needed comfort and support, but it was his suggestion that she spend an evening at church that provided the opportunity for answered prayer. Iris's eyes shine at the mention of the incident: *"I'd been feeling particularly low and didn't know what to do to lift the black cloud of depression. Peter suggested I get dressed and nip down to our local church. The singing and prayers often lifted my spirits."* This time, however, it was what the speaker had to say that made Iris's heart soar.

Slipping quietly into a back seat, she listened as the speaker began to tell the story of a man he'd led to Christ. As he talked, Iris's ears pricked up and her heart began to beat faster. He told of his encounter with an English soldier who was dying in the UVF hospital at Galwally. The tale progressed and eventually he explained how he had read the dying man the wonderful words of John 3:16.

Even the passing of time has not detracted from Iris's joy at the revelation. *"This verse has always been very dear to me but it was the speaker's next words that made my spirit cry out with thanks. I heard him say my father's name. My dad had accepted Christ! He had been saved. He was in glory! God had given me the reassurance I'd craved so long."*

Iris waited to tell the preacher how his words had been the answer to her prayers. Then she ran straight to her mum's house to share her news. When Iris got home that night, television broadcasts may have been full of the Watergate trials, Ian Paisley and Northern Ireland's new Assembly, or the release of the film, *Jesus Christ Superstar*. For Iris Robinson the only topic worth mentioning was the glorious salvation of her 'gentle giant'.

Motherhood may have brought a lot of physical and emotional pain, it was also a time of great blessing. Even the blackest cloud could not stop the rays of God's love from reaching Iris Robinson. The knowledge that her father was safe in the presence of his Lord acted like a balm to her soul. Iris found peace.

8

FULL CIRCLE

JIMMY SAVILLE was making dreams come true with television wizardry and 'Jim'll fix it' badges. In 1976 it was the Northern Ireland Housing Trust that granted Iris Robinson's wish. Almost twenty years after her father's death, Iris, accompanied by Peter and baby Jonathan, moved back to her family home in the Cregagh.

Already a new generation was stamping its identity on everything from politics to fashion. For many, the Seventies lacked the radical impact of the previous decade. The fashion industry failed to replicate the 'wow' factor of the mini skirt. Flared trousers instead of bellbottoms, chiffon scarves and wooden beads suggested variation rather than innovation. Although the Seventies did have something denied to other generations, a heady aroma of Old Spice, Brut, and Charlie perfume, not to mention a craze for curly locks. Instead of Paul

McCartney's Sixties fringe, hairdressers were inundated with demands for Kevin Keegan-style perms.

Mary Collins believed that her home of over thirty years was a lifetime residence. But then, she also thought that her job as an orderly at Forster Green Hospital was simply a source of financial security. The last thing Mary expected to find in the world of hospital monotony was a second chance for happiness! When she met handsome James Malloy, a patient at the hospital, romance blossomed and the couple fell head over heels in love!

When it came to the new man in her mum's life, Iris was delighted! *"Mum deserved a chance to be happy again. When she and James decided to marry, they had my full support. I knew as we all grew up and went our separate ways that life could get lonely for my mum. It was a blessing for them both."*

For Mary, marriage to James meant leaving Belfast for a new home in Portadown. At that time Iris was still struggling with the demands of a toddler and life on the top floor of a three-storey building. Carrying, first a squirming child then his buggy followed by a return trip for shopping was exhausting work! Consequently, after talking it over, everyone agreed that the logical solution was for Iris and Peter to move back to her family home. The Northern Ireland Housing Trust weren't so easy to persuade! Iris soon found she had a battle on her hands. She recalls the struggle: *"I used to carry Jonathan up, leave him, then run back down for the shopping and pram. After his pram was stolen, I was nearing the end of my tether. With mum moving to Portadown it seemed the obvious solution to the problem. However, the Northern Ireland Housing Trust weren't so easily convinced!"*

It took a lot of phone calls, visits, as well as letters, but Iris eventually won her case. She laughs: *"It really was a hard slog but well worth the effort! It was lovely to be in my old home again. We'd lots more space, but I also had lovely memories of my dad. Best of all, Nanny Wylie was right next door! She proved a real blessing to the next generation of our family!"* It has to be said that the experience also equipped Iris for future bureaucratic battles on behalf of others.

Nanny Wylie was equally glad to see Iris back: *"I've known Iris since she came into the world and I couldn't love her more if she were my own daughter. Her family had grown up next door to me and when Iris moved back with Peter and the baby it was a very happy time."*

Outwardly, Iris's life at Cooneen Way appeared to reflect the same patterns of childhood. The dimensions may have altered but family needs and domestic routine were once again her chief priority. Yet there was another aspect to Iris's nature that the intervening years had not altered. Her sense of justice and determination to protect those in need were firmly intact. When Iris returned to Cregagh she discovered that her arena of service extended beyond the family circle. She was now helping Peter take up the problems and struggles of those within their community. Her childhood experiences as well as her knowledge of working-class life became the tools that equipped her for such diversity of work.

As the wife of a newly-elected Councillor, Iris opened her home to the surrounding community who often dropped by with problems or messages for Peter. She chatted, comforted, or used her shorthand skills to make notes for her husband to read later. Before long, as demand grew, the couple put chairs in their hallway and the house began to resemble a surgery more than a home. No one could have envisaged such a scenario, least of all Iris's mum.

Very often, for whatever reason, people would bypass Peter's office on the Albertbridge Road and come straight to their home. The local politician's wife had no problem with the constant, steady stream of visitors. She thought it great that they felt welcome at her home and tried as much as possible to put them at ease. *"I thought it lovely that people felt they could* come to our house. *I wanted them to be comfortable and tried to make them welcome. I'd listen to their problems, take notes, and generally try to reassure them. We took their problems seriously and Peter always did the best he could to find solutions. I think they knew that they could depend on him as his word has always meant something."*

While this was one of the happiest times in the young mum's life, it was often lonely as well as financially difficult. Peter's time was always in heavy demand but Iris reveals an additional pressure: *"Peter had given up a secure job for not only a lower salary, but one that didn't always arrive on time! As any woman in similar circumstances knows, household bills won't wait until a pay cheque arrives. In the early days, the financial side of life was often a bit of a struggle."*

Without a regular income, the young father put in the necessary hours in order to climb his way up the political ladder. Subsequently, the couple endured long separations. With her husband's time at a premium, once again Iris shouldered the responsibility for home and family. She learned that Peter's choice of career meant a heavy workload and few social rewards.

Her friend Hazel knew just how difficult life could be for her. *"Understandably, Peter had to work long hours and Iris was often alone with young Jonathan. Her mum was living in Portadown and sometimes the evenings could get a bit lonely. Occasionally I'd spend a few hours at her house and we'd share the ups and downs of motherhood! It was a hard time for her although, to her credit, she always made the best of the situation."*

Iris may have spent many lonely nights but she had known they would be part and parcel of her married life. The couple had often discussed the direction Peter's career appeared to be heading. Iris understood her husband's passion and dedication. She also shared his desire for peace in Northern Ireland. With such focus and determination, it wasn't a road they could travel lightly. Mrs Robinson was under no illusion about the sacrifices such a life would demand from her. But the knowledge didn't always make it easier.

The situation in Northern Ireland had already reached a crisis. From 1971 to 1972 Northern Ireland's Prime Minister, Brian Faulkner, stumbled his way through what must arguably have been, the worst period of his career. He had introduced internment and witnessed the subsequent event history has recorded as Bloody Sunday. By the time he resigned, Edward Heath, the British Prime Minister, had dissolved Northern Ireland's government and instigated direct rule from London. This infuriated Unionists who felt angry and betrayed. The IRA viewed direct rule as worse than any Stormont government and stepped up its campaign.

That summer added another bloody day in Northern Ireland's history. This time it was a Friday. The detonation of twenty-two no-warning bombs left nine people dead, hundreds injured, and the city of Belfast reeling in shock. With more terrorist groups entering the scene, violence spread and rapidly escalated.

At one point, as sectarianism reached its zenith, families were forced to leave their homes and move to more segregated enclaves. When Catholic neighbours in the estate were targeted, Iris, ever ready to face the bullies, was among the neighbourhood women who defended them. Anger is still evident in her voice: *"I could never condone what happened. The 'thugs' who caused the problems weren't even from our estate. My mum, Nanny Wylie, and many other women stood by our friends and neighbours. I'd grown up with these people and we all stood foursquare behind them. It was a scene that was being played out all over Belfast. It saddened me but at the same time I was furious."*

Iris's sense of fair play and justice has always ensured a healthy disregard for such tactics in any form, whether at street or government level. She still believed in the political route her husband had chosen and endeavoured to fully support him. The cost may have been too much for many young women, but lonely nights and a lack of social life were the sacrifices that Iris was willing to make.

Although reserved by nature, Peter is not shy when it comes to appreciation of his wife: *"I know how difficult it was for Iris, especially in the early days. Very often my work brought fear and a huge amount of stress into our lives. It takes a very special woman to stand beside her husband in such circumstances. Iris is that kind of woman. I know I am richly blessed."*

9

NEW LIFE

THERE WAS nothing Iris liked better than a cup of tea and a chat with her mum. However, the train ride to Portadown was becoming a nightmare – travelling with a toddler and the necessary paraphernalia is not conducive to pleasant journeys. In the end, at twenty-six, Iris decided it was time she learned to drive.

Like many women, her first mistake had nothing to do with gears or clutch control. It was asking her husband for a lesson. When the pair set off, only one of them would return on four wheels. Iris smiles at the memory of the incident: *"I thought Peter would make a good instructor but I quickly realised my mistake!"* The couple set off happily enough but, when Peter ran out of patience, Iris decided to cut the lesson short.

"I was so annoyed that he'd raised his voice that I pulled over, got out of the car, and told him I'd find my own way

home. *I didn't think he'd let me, but he drove off and left me. I was miles from home and I walked all the way, not a bus in sight. That was the end of any driving instructor career for him!"* Iris did eventually pass her test and found that driving provided more than a mode of transport. *"I absolutely loved it! I soon realised that going for a long drive was a great way to beat stress. I think it developed into a form of relaxation therapy!"*

Six years into their marriage and Iris realised that yet another aspect of life was about to be sacrificed. Like other high profile careers, politics is played out in the public arena and it isn't only the party manifesto that is subject to media scrutiny. Personalities are also considered fair game. No area of the politician's life, or that of his family, is exempt from media intrusion.

In the early days, Iris found the loss of privacy a little upsetting. The passing of time has helped, but she can still find it unnerving. *"I'm quite a private person and in the beginning I found media comments really distressing. As Peter began to appear on television, people started to recognise him. I found the curious stares and sometimes the comments overwhelming. Generally speaking, I have to say that most people were genuinely interested and very polite and kind."* Peter, on the other hand, knew exactly how to cope with sarcastic or rude remarks. As succinct as ever, he reveals: *"I grew a thicker hide!"*

Iris may have agreed to share every aspect of her husband's life and, undoubtedly, the couple was and still are very close. Yet, there was one aspect of Iris's life that Peter could not enter. Despite being brought up in a Christian home and knowing the gospel message, he had not accepted Christ as his Saviour. Like all partners of unbelievers, Iris prayed for Peter, and trusted that God would speak to him. At the same time, Mrs Robinson senior was also praying for him. In the fulness of time, God answered the fervent prayers of both his wife and mother.

In 1973 the family had been blessed with the miracle of new life at the birth of baby Jonathan. When Peter Robinson accepted Christ as his personal Saviour, he received the gift of a new and eternal life. Like all who enter into a vital relationship with Christ, Peter remembers his spiritual transaction clearly: *"I was under conviction of sin for some time. My parents had taught us the Scriptures and I knew I needed to be saved but I have a stubborn streak that left me wrestling with the problem for weeks. Eventually I knelt at my bedside and before God I humbly accepted His wonderful gift of salvation."*

Peter's mum and dad were thrilled to learn of their son's conversion. For Iris, it meant that their relationship had entered a new phase of unity. At last, their family had balance. Whatever the young couple planned, they developed the practice of waiting for God's guidance and the final stamp of divine approval. This custom was to become an important part of their daily lives.

In 1977 many believed that Northern Ireland was witnessing the first buds of hope and peace, yet they were not the result of any particular Party's politics. Instead, they were rooted in the tragic deaths of innocent children. Such a loss could not fail to touch the coldest heart. Mothers, in particular, are sensitive and receptive to the pain associated with the death of a child. Yet the loss of innocent life in circumstances of wanton destruction serves only to aggravate the grief. What became known as 'The Peace Movement' organised rallies, speeches, demonstrations, and protests across the Province. Thousands of people armed with placards and baby buggies turned out and demanded an end to violence.

The emotional pleas may have highlighted the grief of people in great mourning, but it did not provide the much sought after solution. The Nobel Prize for Peace was awarded to Mairead Corrigan and Betty Williams but, despite their efforts, the bloodshed continued.

Iris recalls that period with deep sadness: *"It is impossible not to be touched by the loss of innocent children. As a mother, I couldn't begin to imagine the grief. This particular tragedy sparked a gut reaction. Mothers simply wanted an end to violence. I could understand the Peace Movement's motives but I knew that it wasn't the answer."* Iris believes that a lasting solution to Northern Ireland's problems needs a firmer foundation than goodwill or emotion. *"Unfortunately, it's a hard, tough and at times disappointing slog. Yet it's the only route available."*

Three months later the media had turned its attention to other stories. W B Yeats became the first Irish resident on the planet Mercury after scientists named a crater in his honour. Perhaps of most interest to the world was the death of Elvis Presley on 16 August. The subsequent wake of international mourning eclipsed everything else including the news that, just three days after Elvis's death, the famous comedian and actor, Groucho Marx, also entered eternity. Regardless of man's standing in the world, the cycle of life goes on.

Dean Sammy Crooks provided the inspiration for one of Iris's future charity events when he established a Christmas tradition in Northern Ireland culture. Seated outside St Ann's Cathedral in all weathers, the robed figure, known as the 'Black Santa', reminded shoppers of the true spirit of the season. Nearly thirty years later, Iris Robinson carried the same message to one of Belfast's major shopping centres.

10

BLESSINGS AND TRIALS

THE LAST Christmas of the decade must be among the Robinson's family favourites. Whatever Santa brought, he could not compete with Iris's gift, especially to Peter. The young politician may have been used to the more traditional, though colourful, set of matching tie and hanky. But on 30 December 1979, the day after Peter's birthday, Iris gave birth to their second son Gareth.

Memories of her first pregnancy, if not entirely eradicated, had faded enough to allow her to try for another much-wanted baby. She knew from the outset what pregnancy for her would entail. While Iris may have bargained for months of continual nausea, she did not foresee the traumatic and frightening need for surgery just sixteen weeks into her pregnancy. *"I knew I'd be ill, I just didn't know how ill! Peter was absolutely delighted to hear he was going to be a dad again. Yet soon after celebrating our news, I was in agony and we were faced with the very real and terrifying prospect of losing our child."*

Iris was admitted to hospital suffering from suspected appendicitis. Surgery was deemed the only course of action and, naturally enough, the mum-to-be was terrified that she might lose the baby. Mike Crooks, Iris's specialist, did his best to reassure the couple that surgery would not harm their unborn child. Still, when Iris was wheeled into theatre, a few anxious doubts remained. Several hours later Peter and Iris learned the true nature of her diagnosis.

Surgeons did indeed remove her appendix, but the real problem was much more serious and would have repercussions for years to come. The operation revealed that Iris had developed three cysts on an ovary. Worst of all, the couple were told that all three growths had become gangrenous. Thankfully, God used the skill of surgeons as His instrument to bring both mother and baby safely through the ordeal.

After leaving the recovery room, Iris was temporarily placed in a ward full of elderly patients who were suffering from various stages of cancer. With little to fill their day but pain, treatment, and an occasional visitor, Iris soon became a novelty as well as the centre of attention. She smiles as she recalls how the women gathered round for a technological treat. *"Despite assurances that my baby was fine, like most mums can appreciate, I wanted evidence! Mike Crooks asked a nurse to bring a baby monitor so that I could hear the heart beat."*

As time went by and nobody arrived to allay her fear, Iris grew more anxious and stressed. *"On his way through the ward Doctor Crooks noticed me crying. When he discovered that the monitor hadn't arrived, he set off for the maternity ward and brought back the much longed-for equipment! It was a lovely act of kindness for him to go out of his way to put my mind at rest. All the lovely old dears gathered round and listened in amazement to Gareth's heart beat."* It was an incredible moment for those women of a previous generation. Given the same circumstances they would probably have lost both their baby as well as their own life.

If the pregnancy caused the couple a few anxious moments, the birth almost gave Peter a heart attack! In the next cubicle to Iris another Mrs Robinson had given birth to twins. In a confused haze of painkillers Iris absorbed the nurse's congratulations and proceeded to inform a stunned Peter Robinson that he had two babies for the price of one! Iris laughs as she remembers the look on his face: *"Like most men of our generation, Peter wasn't present at any of the births. It was their job to stay in the waiting room where they could do nothing but hang around hoping for news. When Gareth was born I certainly gave him something to think about!"*

1979 may have ended on a note of joy in the Robinson household but terrorism continued to wreak havoc throughout Britain and Ireland. In March the Conservative politician Airey Neave became a victim of terrorism when a bomb exploded in the House of Commons car park. In August the IRA chose a more scenic venue but the carnage was the same. Lord Mountbatten, his fourteen-year-old grandson, Baroness Brabourne, and an innocent local teenager, set off on a sailing trip in Donegal Bay, County Sligo. They had anticipated good company and fair winds, but met only disaster and death.

Politically, British voters were jaded and tired as the Winter of Discontent took its toll. A General Election provided the perfect opportunity for change and so, with a perfect coiffure to match the smile, Margaret Thatcher took up residence at Number 10 and became Britain's first female Prime Minister. Her reputation for having a core of iron soon became her trademark.

Iris Robinson recognised and appreciated many of the woman's qualities. *"I respected Mrs Thatcher and found her to have a number of really good attributes. It isn't easy for a woman to find acceptance in such a male dominated field. Unfortunately, when it came to issues regarding Northern*

Ireland, she listened to and acted on what turned out to be some really bad advice."

It wasn't only Mrs Thatcher who celebrated an election victory. May 1979 was a very special time for the Robinson family. After years of hard work Peter had not only earned the confidence of his constituents, he had won their votes. With the last one counted, it was clear that the people of East Belfast had decided that Peter Robinson should represent them at Parliament. As his greatest supporter, Iris was delighted. *"It was a fantastic moment when Peter was elected to Parliament! He had worked hard and people knew from experience that he was someone they could trust."*

As Parliamentary duties increased, so did Peter's absences from home. Iris had been used to her husband's unpredictable hours but at least, no matter how late, she could look forward to his return in the evening. The necessity for overnight stays in London not only added to Iris's loneliness, but robbed Peter of time with his family.

As a Christian, Iris clung to her faith but missed the support and warmth that is found in the continuity of fellowship. Like many young Christian mums she found that the hustle and bustle of daily life made too many inroads on her time. After getting two young children fed, bathed, and into bed, never mind asleep, attending the local Bible study isn't always an easy option, even if there just happens to be a babysitter ready and available. Yet, as she later discovered, God understands the various problems that beset every season of life. They may hinder us but they never thwart His plan.

Iris may not have realised it at the time but God had a purpose for her. It is only the gift of hindsight that allows us to see the divine hand that has guided, directed, and encouraged us along His path. Rearing children, listening to the problems of her community, and taking a back seat whilst supporting her husband may have, to an onlooker, seemed mundane. But it was all part of the divine training for her future role in helping others.   While her time was occupied with the demands of domesticity, God was already preparing Iris's spiritual field of service. Some of the people, who would one day be her spiritual guides as well as family, had not as yet even met the Lord. The decade was a time of sowing and preparing for the harvest to come.

Meanwhile, the world at large fretted and worried about the ozone layer and climatic extremes. When snow fell in the Sahara Desert it seemed that Sweden's decision to ban aerosols and prevent further atmospheric damage was well founded. Ireland's freezing temperature of -18C, the lowest of the century, only added to concerns. Even Sunday sermons began to adopt an ecological theme as some ministers exhorted their flock on the necessity of good stewardship on earth.   At Whitewell Metropolitan Church in North Belfast the only topic on Pastor McConnell's agenda was salvation. Already, the church that would one day feature so prominently in the Robinson's spiritual life, was finding their nets full and overflowing!

While God prepared a place for both Iris and Peter at Whitewell, the woman who would become most instrumental in Iris's life and Christian service was right under her nose.

11

SACRIFICES

WHATEVER WAS on the New Year lunch menu at 10 Downing Street, Mrs Thatcher started the decade with a political hot potato. The National Steel Industry's decision to strike may have tempered her appetite but it also set the theme for the rest of the year. Across the Atlantic, American President Jimmy Carter had his own problems. With over a billion dollars worth of loans, the peanut farmer turned politician attempted to rescue the Chrysler Corporation. No matter how interesting or curious current world events are, it is the circumstances within our individual spheres that are always most important.

While the Prime Minster wrestled with problems on a national scale, thirty-year-old Iris Robinson had her own domestic blips. By 1980 Peter had taken on the role of Deputy Leader of the Democratic Unionist Party. With one primary school child plus the demands of a new baby, life at home was hard work. Yet Iris was used to the routine and, although she continued to miss him, understood the need for her husband's frequent absences.

She explains how Peter's vision for the DUPs future success demanded one hundred percent commitment. *"Anyone who knows Peter will understand the kind of man he is. He is totally focused and committed to his work. He was determined that the Party should have the success it deserved and that he would play his part. It did mean long hours and missing out on a lot of family life but I'm not complaining, we both knew that would be one of the prices. Although I have to admit, sometimes it was no picnic!"* Of course, Iris wasn't home alone every night. Her friend Hazel and sister Marlene often dropped by. When in need of some sisterly advice or a mug of tea, her brothers also called in.

Raising a young family requires an unlimited amount of energy but Iris was beginning to notice that her reserves were fast running out. Once again cysts and gynaecological problems were making her life an absolute misery. Hospital admissions occurred with frightening regularity as Iris underwent one horrific procedure after another. *"It really was a terrible time. I think at one point I had been admitted seventeen times!"*

One of the worst procedures was when surgeons attempted to lift and suspend her womb, leaving Iris in agony as well as tears. Piece by piece her ovaries were removed but she was determined to have one last attempt to add a daughter to her blessings. *"My gynaecologist, Mike Crooks, was wonderful. He knew how much I wanted to try for a daughter. We adored our sons but it seemed that a little girl would complete the family. My womb and ovaries were in a dreadful state but he helped me to hang on as long as possible."*

While doctors did their best to alleviate her pain, Iris had another source of comfort. *"No matter when I was in hospital, God always sent along a Christian man or woman to pray with me. He never failed me although there were times when I was so low I certainly failed Him."*

While Iris struggled with her condition, she continued with the exhausting routine of looking after home and family as well as the regular visits from Peter's constituents. Like most young families who encounter ill health or some other unexpected intrusion in life, the couple did their best to carry on as normally as possible. Peter continued to appear on television, speak at press conferences, and push his Party's political agenda. In between, even in London, he was dashing to the phone for a quick progress report. He made sure he offered his own prescription of tender loving care. During these times Iris never felt neglected. *"No matter how busy, Peter made sure he contacted or visited me. Come to think of it, I saw more of him when I was in hospital than at home!"*

However, life, whether in the political or public domain, doesn't allow much room for private problems. Peter remembers those days when his heart and head engaged in a kind of tug of war. Instinctively, he knew his place should be at Iris's bedside. Yet common sense and logic dictated that, at such a sensitive time in Northern Ireland politics, work responsibilities should take priority.

Peter takes up the story: *"I knew that things were particularly difficult for Iris. Pregnancy was never easy for her. She was dreadfully sick for much of the time. I worried constantly about her."* After a moment's reflection, he adds: *"If I'm honest I have to say I also felt a huge amount of guilt. She hadn't chosen the kind of life where her husband would be in London for a great deal of the time. In fact, neither of us realised the full impact politics would have on our private lives."*

As the Party grew and expanded it was inevitable that Peter's responsibilities would encroach on their time together. However, he believed it worthwhile. *"I really thought that my efforts could help change and shape a better life for our kids as well as future generations. I can't say I didn't enjoy the work, for I did; it was exciting and challenging and I found a great deal of satisfaction."* With hindsight Peter is quick to recognise the downside that had repercussions for the whole family. *"Not being there meant they missed out on a normal family life but I too missed so much."*

Regardless of personal consequences, Peter knew he had Iris's full support. He also knew that she wasn't completely alone. His young brother-in-law had continued to live with them after Iris's mum remarried and moved to Portadown. Iris explains: *"When mum moved to Portadown, my brother was torn between going with her and his life in Belfast. He enjoyed living in the city and it seemed a good idea to offer him a home with us. Peter and he got on well and I liked having him around. It was like old times!"*

Very often the young man helped his sister by amusing six-year-old Jonathan while Iris fed or dressed baby Gareth. Iris's other brothers and sister continued to call at the house. In fact, their visits were so regular that it seemed as though the only difference was that the family had extended to include Peter and a new generation of Robinsons!

At one time it had been Iris who proved such a blessing to her widowed mum. As a child she had shouldered much of the family responsibility enabling her mother to work. But when Iris was ill and needed hospitalisation, the blessing rebounded in the shape of Mary Malloy. She didn't hesitate to return to Belfast to care for her son-in-law and grandchildren. Both Iris and Peter are tremendously grateful.

Iris smiles as she recalls her mum's generosity: *"I could never thank her enough for being there for us. When I needed help she would pack a bag, leave her new husband in Portadown, and come to our house to look after Peter and the kids."* Peter adds his own comments: *"My mother-in-law was absolutely brilliant when Iris was ill and the kids were so young. I don't know what I'd have done without her. She certainly took a lot of worry off my mind. I was able to get on with things at work, visit Iris, and know that the kids were okay with their granny."*

For Iris, the pain and disruption of ill health may have seemed unnecessary and useless. However, her belief that God has a purpose for everything provided much solace. She considered it part of His plan and when the time came for Iris to comfort others, she would be able to draw from a deep well of compassion.

By the end of the year, the news was filled with the death of John Lennon. His life was cut short and the voice that had earned millions silenced as the singer was unexpectedly gunned down outside his home in New York. People talked and wondered at the madness of such a chaotic, uncertain world. But, within a few days, they returned to the safe complacency of anonymity and routine. Iris and Peter may have lived in an ordinary house in Cregagh, they may not have had the recognition and fame of the former Beatle but at one point they were just as vulnerable.

The decade had introduced a new sacrifice to Iris's life. Security had become a very real issue. No longer were Iris's sleepless nights due to baby Gareth's colic or teething problems. The threat of terrorism had become up-close and personal. Almost three decades had elapsed since Iris Collins lost her 'gentle giant' but once again death lurked at her shoulder ready to snatch those at the centre of her world. The intervening years may have provided a cloak of maturity to help develop a coping mechanism but, for Iris Robinson, it did nothing to remove the fear.

12

COURAGEOUS WOMEN

IF THE previous year's industrial action caused Mrs Thatcher a headache, the Republican hunger strikes of 1981 at Northern Ireland's Maze Prison had all the ingredients for a political migraine. As the prisoners began to refuse food in a bid to achieve political status, few guessed where the situation would lead. Weeks passed as the government maintained a negative stance and the protest continued.

Eventually, on 5 May, Bobby Sands became the first of ten prisoners to die from self-imposed starvation. The political atmosphere was electric. Prior to his death, voters had elected the IRA member as MP for Fermanagh and South Tyrone, adding a completely new dimension to Northern Ireland's political scene. Once again violence erupted. This time it wasn't only the streets of Belfast that witnessed the upsurge, demonstrations outside the British Embassy in Dublin quickly turned hostile and violent.

For most of the residents of Cregagh the violent repercussions of current events could be turned off with a flick of a switch. Although, for the family at 16 Cooneen Way, refusing to watch the television images would not lessen the threat. It isn't easy to live with the knowledge that death could be lurking round the next corner. Iris frowns as she tries to put her feelings into words: *"It's almost impossible to convey what it's like to live with fear. You look over your shoulder the whole time. Every situation has an element of suspicion."*

The knowledge that someone you dearly love is considered a target for violence is a terrifying experience. At that particular time Iris wasn't personally involved with politics which in a way made it worse. *"When something bad happened, I didn't know any more than anyone else. I had to wait until Peter could get to a phone and reassure me. We lived in an ordinary terraced house which I really loved but death threats made life increasingly stressful as we had very little security at the time."*

While most headlines made depressing reading, the summer managed to offer a little light relief. On 29 July Charles and Diana became the nation's favourite newlyweds. In fact, it was a wedding that Iris Robinson did not want to miss. *"Like everyone else at the time I was enchanted by what seemed to be a fairytale romance. There was a great sense of fun and excitement in the days leading up to the wedding and I decided I'd like to be part of it."*

She talked it over with Peter and they came to the conclusion that there was only one thing to do! Iris would go to the wedding! *"Although there was no four star hotel room waiting, my friend and I camped on the pavement and had an absolute ball! The atmosphere was buzzing as we all chatted and laughed in anticipation of the Big Day!"* Of course, the future tragedy was still shrouded in mystery. Only God knew the fate that awaited the young princess. The wedding ceremony, the bridal dress, and the line-up of international guests provided media fodder for weeks to come. Iris sums it all up in a few words: *"She was simply gorgeous."*

Whatever 1981 contributed to history, in the Robinsons' opinion it was the year of their own little miracle! After numerous medical procedures and complications Iris had been left with just one ovary. But in November she was thrilled to learn that they were expecting another child. Still barely able to conceal her joy at the memory, she explains: *"It was an incredible moment when I told Peter and the family that baby number three was on the way. With just one ovary, my chances of conceiving were reduced by half. Nevertheless, nothing is impossible with God. With my history, I knew it wasn't going to be an easy pregnancy but I was determined to have one last try for a daughter."*

Her forecast of pregnancy sickness turned out to be completely accurate. If anything, she had underestimated the physical cost of another baby. Almost from the moment of conception, Iris was severely and constantly ill. Less than three months into her pregnancy, she was admitted to hospital and began the familiar routine of scans, baby monitors, and intravenous drips. Yet, despite the pain, distress, and temporary disruptions to daily life, the couple knew that a healthy baby would make it all worthwhile.

Whatever Iris expected that year, there was one scenario she had not foreseen. Prostrate on a hospital bed, trying hard to ignore the persistent waves of nausea, she happened to overhear a nurse's hurried and urgent conversation. Rushing into the ward, the young woman brought news of Northern Ireland's latest victim of terrorism. Iris's heart almost failed as she heard that Peter Robinson had been killed.

She recalls her panic: *"As soon as I heard the victim's name, I'm sure I came close to a heart attack. I'll never forget the moment when I learned that Peter had been shot dead. My worst fears had come true. I just had to get to him, so, without thinking, I pulled out the drips, jumped out of bed, and began running out of the hospital."* Nurses tried to calm their hysterical patient but a phone call and a familiar voice proved the only remedy. Eventually medical staff managed to convince Iris that Peter was okay and was actually on the phone waiting to talk to her.

"O, the relief that flooded through me! As soon as I heard Peter's voice, I knew that I'd been spared the tragedy that had arrived at another family's door. Peter's voice was choked with emotion as he told me that Robert Bradford had just been murdered. Immediately my heart went out to Nora. I understood a little of the feeling she was about to experience at the news of her husband's death."

Peter was stunned by Robert's death and found it difficult to come to terms with the fact that he'd lost yet another friend to mindless terrorism. *"Robert and I had become good friends,"* he explains. *"We'd spent a lot of time together planning a propaganda tour, known as Operation USA. We intended to use the book 'Ulster, The Facts' to show the American people the reality of terrorism. It was vital that those who supported or financed the IRA understood the devastation and human suffering their campaign inflicted. We also wanted to portray the true Unionist position."*

Peter goes on to tell how his first thoughts were for Nora, Robert's wife. *"I rang Nora immediately but it was obvious from her tone that she hadn't heard of her husband's death and as I'd learned from an unofficial source, I couldn't tell her. To be honest, I really wouldn't have wanted to be the one to give such devastating news."*

When Peter rang off, Nora's world was, for a little while, still intact. His next call was to Iris, where he could find, as well as offer, comfort. However, when Peter rang the hospital he learned that his wife had also suffered a shock. *"I was really concerned for Iris as well as the baby. The way in which she'd learned of her dad's death had left an emotional scar. To learn of mine in a similar manner would add an additional pain. I'd intended to sound calm and reassuring but as soon as I heard her voice, it was impossible to hide my distress and my poor wife ended up trying to comfort me."*

A few weeks later, thanks to the support of two courageous women, Peter was in America on the first lap of the tour. His admiration for both his wife and Mrs Bradford is obvious. *"There aren't many women who could support their husband in such circumstances. Iris is one of the few and, regardless of the personal inconvenience, encouraged me to go ahead with the American trip. When Nora Bradford decided to go in her husband's place, I was amazed at her bravery and courage."*

Even a crowd of angry NORAID demonstrators outside their hotel didn't bother either Peter or Mrs Bradford. When the taxi driver asked if they'd like to use a back entrance or walk through the protesters, they chose the latter. Peter adds: *"Nora and I walked straight past, they didn't know us at all!"* The tour continued as Robert and Peter had planned. In spite of protests, threats, and even bomb scares, they got their message across. Frequent calls home kept Iris up to date with all the news. In the early days, the telephone was their main form of communication. While it certainly kept the couple in touch, it was no substitute for actually being there.

Back in Belfast the death of Robert Bradford sparked an upgrade of security for the Robinsons in Cooneen Way. The bulletproof windows may have offered the family a certain amount of reassurance, although for Iris Robinson they were a constant, tangible reminder that her family's lives were in danger.

13

FAMILY AFFAIRS

WHATEVER NEWS the DUPs Deputy Leader expected on 15 May 1982 there was one call he didn't want to miss. When the much anticipated news arrived, everything else paled in comparison. Six months after losing his friend and the inevitable sadness that followed, Peter Robinson's world shone with happiness. Already blessed with two sons, Iris presented him with a baby daughter and in the process completely ruined his reputation as Mr Cool.

As the proud father cradled his daughter in his arms it was impossible to wipe the grin from his face! His first impression of his little girl can be summed up in one word. Twenty-four years on and the dad is just as proud, his grin as wide, and the adjective the same ... *"Beautiful!"*

It wasn't just Peter who showed his delight when the little lady arrived. Iris recounts how the delivery suite was in an uproar of celebrations! *"As soon as Rebekah was born, the atmosphere in the delivery suite was incredible! Mike Crooks and the nurses literally jumped around with delight! Everyone knew how much this baby meant to me and shared my happiness."*

Iris knew it was likely to be her last pregnancy and to have a little girl would complete her family. Long before she'd even been conceived, Iris had already chosen her daughter's name. *"I met a wonderful Christian woman named Rebekah who impressed me greatly. I always said that if ever I had a little girl she too would share this lovely biblical name. God had already blessed us with two marvellous boys but our daughter's birth was a welcome addition and brought the year to a close with thanksgiving and praise."*

With their family complete the couple returned to the business of daily life. For Peter it meant an endless round of meetings and public engagements, trying to ensure that his constituents were happy with their political representative. Three-year-old Gareth also did his bit! Already a firm favourite with the older ladies, the little lad entertained and charmed his way into their affections. No doubt, more than a few crosses beside the DUP candidate's name on the ballot paper were instigated by toddler Robinson! His mum, thrilled with her new daughter, tried desperately to ignore the continuing problems with her health.

Peter's political career was causing Iris more than a few sleepless nights. An unexpected phone call late at night was enough to set her heart racing. Television images of a car bomb in an area where she knew Peter was likely to be would set the adrenaline pumping. Like all who live with the fear of violence, Iris experienced every spectrum of emotion. Unlike his wife, Peter had learned early to develop a coping mechanism and managed to control his emotional response. But there is one place where both are equally vulnerable. The armour of cool objectivity doesn't work in the tender area of parental love. Our children are the weakest link in even the strongest psyche.

When Iris's brother called to share his delight at becoming a dad, a loud bang shattered the celebratory mood. Meanwhile Peter, returning from work, was met by the sight of a familiar bicycle lying on the ground in a tangled heap. Beside it lay his ten-year-old son Jonathan. Fearing the worst, Peter rushed to the boy, taking in at a glance his numerous injuries. He recalls the image that all parents dread: *"I was first to get to Jonathan and I dreaded, but at the same time, needed to understand the nature of his injuries. It was easy to see my son was badly hurt and I couldn't even begin to describe my emotions. Only a parent who has been in the situation can appreciate the feelings involved. There's an overwhelming need to protect against further pain. We want to try to make the problem go away."*

Unlike Peter, Iris's response has always been more outwardly emotional and the sight of her injured son evoked a hysterical reaction. *"When I heard the bang, I knew immediately there'd been an accident. Yet for some reason I didn't think of Jonathan straight away. We'd been so careful to warn them of our security situation that I just assumed safety was always their top priority but you can't legislate against accidents. Neither can you wrap kids in cotton wool and protect them from all the nasty things in life."*

As soon as Iris stepped out the front door and saw one of her neighbours running with a blanket, she asked who had been injured. The woman's expression said it all and Iris knew it was her son. Screaming, she ran to the scene to find Peter cradling the little broken body. In quiet reassuring tones, he managed to calm both wife and child as they waited for an ambulance to arrive. *"It was obvious from the way Jonathan's leg was bent beneath him that it was badly broken. Clumps of his hair had come out and his head was bleeding. My heart ached when he*

looked up and asked if he was going to die. That was one of the
worst moments of my life."
    Thankfully, the Lord spared the young lad but he was very
badly injured. In fact, such were the extent of his injuries that
he was unable to return to school for the next year. Jonathan
remembers the disappointment as well as the pain vividly. But
he also remembers a slightly strange and inexplicable slant to
the scenario.
    Now thirty-three years old, Jonathan takes up the story:
"There are many things I recall about the accident, like lots of
pain and endless hospital visits. One thing that is really
peculiar is the fact that the day before I was knocked down, I
actually predicted the event! In school we were asked to write
an essay on any subject we liked. I wrote about an imaginary
incident where I was playing on my friend's bike, the brakes
failed, and I got knocked down! Next day, fiction became
reality!" If Jonathan is ever tempted to write about himself
again, no doubt he'll choose a much happier ending!
    His year's absence from primary school had a knock-on
effect. After missing so much of his education, Jonathan didn't
pass his 11+ examination and, therefore, didn't meet the
necessary criteria for entrance to grammar school. It was a
source of frustration for the young man. Knowing their son's
intellectual ability and school preference, Iris and Peter decided
the best course of action was to enrol him as a boarder at a local
grammar school.
    Both mother and son had mixed feelings about the
prospect. Iris recalls how, for the first few weeks, she developed
a severe bout of 'neurotic mother syndrome!' *"The school policy*
was that children should have a few days to settle before any
traumatic reunions with tearful mums. I was beside myself
with apprehension! I absolutely plagued the school with calls
asking after Jonathan. Eventually the matron called a spade
'a spade' and told me that I was worrying needlessly. My son
was as happy as a pig in muck!"

By the time Jonathan was thirteen he was able to sit the common entrance exams which he passed with flying colours and was able to return to the more normal 'day boy' status. But, like the rest of his siblings, his school days often offered more than a few unhappy moments. As with most kids, school had its good and bad days. Boarding may have made him much more independent; it was, however, at times difficult. *"By and large I got on with most people but there were a few times when some certainly showed their dislike of the Robinson name! Still, it was nothing I couldn't handle by myself. Although, I have to say, I wouldn't like my own children to board as it's fairly open to bullying. I was just luckier than most."*

As parents, Peter and Iris realised that their children would be exposed to taunts and bullying. *"It's a fact of life,"* Peter explains, *"that children of all high profile parents, whatever their field, will be subjected to a lot more unwelcome attention than most. The school playground can be a cruel and merciless arena. We tried to equip our kids with the skills necessary to survive such an environment. However, it's always difficult to accept when our children are the innocent casualties of parental choices."*

Bullying is a subject that has always raised Iris's temperature. Her distaste for it at whatever level, whether in the playground or the work place, is evident. *"Even as a child, I tried to stand against such cowardly tactics. I knew that our kids would come in for their fair share of nasty comments simply because of their name but, when gathered around the dinner table one evening and their stories came tumbling out, I was amazed at the cruelty they'd suffered. Yet, I am so proud of how they handled each situation. They are incredibly strong. Maybe they all got their dad's thick hide!"*

14

NIGHT OUT

WHEN PETER Robinson told Sammy Wilson that he'd just ordered Herman out of his home, Belfast's former Lord Mayor was speechless! His friend's direct approach was well known but the Chief Constable of the RUC must have committed a serious misdemeanour to warrant such an inhospitable reception.

Sammy laughs as he recalls the incident: *"Herman turned out to be Iris and Peter's Old English Sheep Dog, absolutely gorgeous, but far too big for the house!"* While Peter stayed home and tried his hand at training Herman, he made the mistake of sending Iris to choose a kennel. She returned with what was definitely a doggy palace! Sammy chuckles at how Peter phoned with an unusual request. *"I thought I was hearing things when Peter asked if I could help get a dog's kennel into their garden. How big could it possibly be? In fact, it turned out to be enormous! True to character, Iris had gone overboard and chosen the biggest kennel she could find!"*

By the time their friend arrived, the Robinson family had given up the struggle. Herman's elaborate home was sitting in the street while everyone, including the dog, looked on in amusement. Unable to offer a solution, Sammy joined the perplexed group. *"We all stood about wondering what to do, when suddenly one of the policemen who was with us suggested we haul it over the roof! It seemed a great idea, so he rushed home and came back with all the necessary tools including a ladder."* Ten minutes later Sammy was up on the roof hauling one end of a rope that was attached to a very heavy load. *"What a job! Pulling that huge doggie house over the roof and down the other side was back breaking work"* he says. *"Come to think of it, I seem to recall that Peter was doing all the supervising!"*

The incident made a hilarious spectacle for onlookers as well as those involved. But it is only one of many anecdotes that reveal a good-natured humour to the couple's private life. Peter's dry wit and Iris's mischievous sense of fun is well known in their circle of friends and close family.

Sammy remembers with amusement the time when he and Iris vetoed Peter's preference for a quiet meal at a local restaurant for a more lively evening at Belfast's popular Group Theatre. After half-an-hour Sammy wished they'd listened to Peter and opted for dinner instead of derision! *"We were trying to decide where to spend the evening and Peter's choice of a quiet meal didn't appeal. Iris certainly enjoys good food but her bubbly personality also appreciates a lively atmosphere. She knows how to make people feel at ease and is good company."*

After a moment's reflection, Sammy reveals another aspect of his friend's character that makes her so special. *"I think one of the nice things about Iris is that she doesn't follow the trend. She's not afraid to be herself even if it goes against the grain of conformity. I like her down-to-earth attitude."*

Regardless of what the group expected from their night at the theatre, it was not an amusing experience. *"We wanted something different,"* Sammy Wilson laughs. *"We certainly got it!"* The Group Theatre was a fairly popular venue offering various acts and skits about life in Belfast. The friends didn't know what was on that night but assumed that fun would be a major ingredient. *"We all headed for the theatre and settled ourselves for a good night out. Well, it turned out that the programme that evening had a real Republican flavour! As soon as they realised that three DUP reps were in the audience we became the butt of the jokes and took some real stick! You can imagine our discomfort! Still, we sat it out and took it on the chin, but we weren't in a hurry back!"*

Apart from her natural sense of humour and zest for life, Iris has a more profound trait in her character. An overwhelming love for her family and especially toward Peter is the foundation of her life. It has also, on numerous occasions, proved a painful Achilles heel. Her Christian faith provides direction and influences her choices but love for the partner God provided adds colour and meaning to her life. *"Like most married couples we've had difficult times, especially with our particular circumstances, yet Peter's love and support have never wavered. When a union is from God, love is easy, comfortable, and very deep. It spans the years and matures with us. Yet it's easy, as with all our blessings, to take a good relationship for granted."*

Apart from her faith, there's nothing Iris loves to talk about more than her family. Motherhood has brought enormous joy. As most mums know, it can also give a few painful stings. *"It's hard to watch our kids go through their own trials and know there's nothing we can do to help."* Like many parents, Iris has

Iris's Father, Joseph Collins, the 'Gentle Giant'

Iris's Mother, Mary Collins

Iris as a toddler

Iris's Stepfather, James Malloy

*Iris as a pupil of Knockbreda
Intermediate School*

Iris and friends at Cregagh Technical College, 1966

Iris and Peter in 1966

Iris and Peter as teenagers in love

Iris youth hostelling at Silver Strand, Ireland

Iris on a secretary appreciation day

Iris and Peter on their Wedding Day

Peter's first Council electioneering photograph

Best friends, Iris with Hazel Pickervance

Peter with sons Jonathan and Gareth at home in Cooneen Way

Iris with daughter Rebekah at 16 Cooneen Way

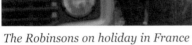

The Robinsons on holiday in France   *Gareth Robinson aged 3*

Sons Jonathan and Gareth with 'Herman' the sheep dog

Iris meeting Peter on his release from Crumlin Road Prison

Iris and Peter being introduced to Princess Diana

Jonathan and Angie's wedding on the day of the Omagh bombing

Iris with James McConnell at her son's wedding

Peter feeding 'Elsie' the Koi Carp

Peter and his 50th Birthday tie

The Robinsons - Iris and Peter, sons Jonathan and Gareth, daughter Rebekah, daughter-in-law Angie, grandchildren Michael and Olivia

Peter with grandson Michael

Peter with granddaugher Olivia

*Iris with Prince Andrew at the official opening of the
Castlereagh Borough Council Offices*

*George Best with Peter Robinson and Adrian Donaldson at
Castlereagh Borough Council*

Iris at the Dundonald Ice Bowl

Iris and colleagues outside her Strangford Constituency Office

Iris, inspired by Dean Crooks, carries out Christmas charity work

Iris at Strangford Lough in 2001

often felt an acute sense of inadequacy at not being able to shield their two sons and daughter from life's sorrows. It doesn't matter how grown-up our children may be, the maternal bond is always there. *"We always want to nurture and protect our kids. Even with Peter, I find the urge to protect equally as strong. It can be hard for me when his work and dedication doesn't get the deserved recognition. He never seeks centre stage and is happy to let others take the credit. However, I don't think I'm much different to many other wives and mothers!"*

Iris's sister Marlene believes that Iris's passion for family is rooted in her childhood. When she took on a mothering role at just six years of age, it set the pattern for life. *"Iris was our protector and champion. We were her family and she looked after us. When Peter came along, her family simply enlarged. They really are fortunate because there aren't many couples who could have taken the stress that has been handed to them."*

Sammy Wilson agrees that the strength of Iris's emotion is also her weakness. *"Politics can be hard and cruel. It must be gratifying to know that there's always a warm welcome waiting at home. For Iris, such strength of emotion has its drawbacks. She and Peter work in an area filled with barbs. They will always come under attack and Iris's one 'fault' is her sensitivity. She does and will continue to get hurt."*

In the mid-Eighties two incidents occurred that had a profound effect on Iris's life. One was due to divine grace when God saved her sister-in-law Pat and filled Iris's life with joy. *"When Pat told me she'd been saved, praise and thanks just bubbled within me. This was something my mother-in-law had prayed about for a long time."* Pat is equally delighted by the new bond with her sister-in-law. *"Until I gave my life to the Lord, Iris and I were like any other sisters-in-law, related simply by marriage. But from the moment I told her I was saved, she was thrilled and a new thread bound us together.*

*No longer just in-laws, we were sisters in the family of Christ.
It is a wonderful relationship."*

Whatever joy the two women shared in their Christian
fellowship, neither had any idea how God would bring them
even closer. Throughout her walk with God, Iris had secretly
longed to serve in the ministry of music. Pat was the instrument
that God would use to bring that desire to fruition. The second
event that was to prove so traumatic had a more natural origin.
Iris had to deal with the difficulties following Peter's arrest at
Clontibret and his subsequent trial in Dublin.

15

TROUBLED TIMES

1985 DAWNED to the familiar sound of church bells, car horns, and Hogmanay cheers. In a rapidly evolving era of technology, it was little wonder that a new note should join the cacophony. On 1 January the comedian Ernie Wise made Britain's first mobile phone call to Vodafone thereby launching a new generation of telecommunications. In coming years such gadgets would prove a necessary accessory. At that time mobile phones were a luxury item. Teenagers, in particular, had not yet traded the grammatically correct for an abbreviated but faster language known as 'text messages'.

While technology continued to upgrade society with personal computers and home entertainment systems, scientists warned of a possible meltdown. A hole in the ozone layer, first suspected in 1977, was finally confirmed and, in an effort to guard against further damage, the recycling campaign got under way.

In spite of technological advances and scientific predictions, for people in the North and South of Ireland, it was the political events of 15 November 1985 that presented a major topic of conversation. Prime Minister Margaret Thatcher and Taoiseach Dr Garret Fitzgerald signed the Anglo Irish Agreement and ignited a political inferno.

The motive may have been to win Nationalist support while protecting the interests of Unionists, the net result was a backlash of violence and a deep-rooted sense of betrayal. Republicans rejected it on the basis that it confirmed Northern Ireland's status within the UK, while horrified Unionists felt utterly betrayed. Their exclusion from pre-Agreement talks was a bitter pill to swallow and only served to heighten the feeling of alienation.

Mary Robinson, later to become President of the Republic of Ireland, shared the Unionist sentiments to such an extent that she resigned from the Irish Labour Party in protest. Iris showed her appreciation by sending the future president a letter of thanks. In Britain, the Conservative Monday Club's spokesman was still publicly condemning the Agreement as late as September 1989. In fact, the only obvious support stemmed from the more moderate SDLP and cross-community Alliance Party.

In an attempt to demonstrate the depth of opposition against the Agreement, all fifteen of Northern Ireland's Unionist MPs resigned. In an act of solidarity both the DUP and UUP organised what became known as the *Ulster Says No* campaign. By using mass rallies, strikes, civil disobedience, and a protest petition with over 400,000 signatures, they ensured the Unionist voice spoke loud and clear. As a consequence, both Loyalist and Republican terrorist groups increased their level of violence.

For Iris Robinson, politics had become a way of life. At seventeen she knew as much about party manifestos and electoral procedures as her contemporaries did about fashion and music. It was simply another subject in her rapidly expanding world. Almost twenty years later, fifteen of them married to a high profile politician, it was little wonder that the subject should still feature so prominently.

When 1985 ushered in the Anglo Irish Agreement, politics suddenly took on a more personal note for Iris – it became the catalyst that propelled her from behind the scenes to front stage politics. Instead of an active supporter, Iris now wanted to take part in the game. *"There was a real sense of betrayal and anger. People found it impossible to accept. I was really disappointed when people like John Hume made insensitive comments about why Unionists were excluded. I knew that the outside world would listen to the SDLP leader and possibly be swayed by him. It certainly made the Unionist view even more difficult to explain abroad."*

As well as political factors, for Iris there was also a more personal element. Once again her thoughts returned to the loss of her dad. *"My dad died from illnesses contracted while fighting for democracy. I wondered what he'd make of the Agreement and knew he would never approve."* For Iris the events of 1985 proved a definite watershed as she determined to become more involved with local politics. However, as a Christian, she needed some divine direction.

"I'm a fairly emotional woman so I know the value of being able to wait for God's guidance. It isn't easy but, nonetheless, it is essential. Whether or not I had a role in politics became a matter of prayer. It was a question that only God could answer." God did supply the answer but, as with the confirmation of her dad's salvation, it was in His time. Four years later to be exact. In the meantime, Iris joined with Ulster and said 'No' to the Anglo Irish Agreement. She took part in the

demonstrations and rallies, and even refused to pay her car tax, a decision that would ultimately land her in prison.

However, it wasn't only political frustration that Iris battled. Ill health continued to plague her. After the birth of Rebekah her health went from bad to worse. Despite a variety of medical interventions, she found herself barely able to get through the day. Although Iris didn't realise it, she was suffering from a severe lack of oestrogen and at just thirty-four was already experiencing an early onset of the menopause.

Iris's own diagnosis proved far off the mark. *"I thought I needed a tonic! Eventually I became so seriously ill that I had to have a hysterectomy. Surgeons decided to leave a small piece of ovary to prevent the full onslaught of menopausal symptoms."*

Despite post-operative tenderness, Iris was determined to take part in the protest at the City Hall. She found it a sensitive occasion in more ways than one. *"My delicate state wasn't up to the man-handling that took place that day!"*

A year later the Unionist answer to the Anglo Irish Agreement was still an emphatic 'No'! Despite the disruption of strikes and protests the people of Northern Ireland stalwartly continued with the business of daily life. For the Robinson's, health may have improved but security had become a major issue. Their home in Cregagh, at one time an informal constituency office, was potentially a relatively easy terrorist target.

Peter recalls the worsening threat to his family's safety: *"Everyone within political circles was a potential target but we all learned to live with the threat. The issue of security was always current and sometimes it was necessary to make the odd adjustment. We both loved our home in Cooneen Way; Iris, in particular, had her roots there. When we were advised that the task of securing it properly was proving impossible and that our family as well as neighbours were vulnerable to attack, we had to be realistic. It was time to move."*

Of course, there were those who believed the couple's decision had more to do with prestige than with protection – the implication being that a house in a working-class estate was no longer good enough for their elevated social status. Both Iris and Peter regard such criticism as unfair as well as hurtful. They insist that leaving Cooneen Way was a painful experience for them all. Iris sighs as she explains: *"My roots were in that house. All my memories were there. Of course I didn't want to leave. Such accusations were untrue. Whether Mayor or MP it didn't matter to us, it was our home, we knew everyone and we loved it."*

The hard facts would not go away – violence in Northern Ireland had escalated. The couple had experienced some really frightening and upsetting incidents. Funeral wreaths with Peter's name on them had been sent to the house. His obituary even appeared in the *Belfast Telegraph* and the threat of violence was mounting daily.

When they were informed that terrorists could use either Nanny's or another neighbour's home to get to Peter, and there was no way to secure it, Iris agreed they had to go. When the family moved a few miles up the road to Dundonald their security improved. Although, as Iris reveals, the sight of panic buttons, cameras, and bodyguards really brought their precarious situation well and truly home.

Despite missing the familiarity of her old home and familiar faces, the new house did offer a few exciting challenges. *"I began to indulge my passion for interior design! Peter, with every spare moment he got, set about whipping the garden into shape and eventually managed to create an interest for himself and the lads as well as a home for a horde of Japanese Koi fish!"*

In 1986 Peter became Castlereagh's Mayor and his responsibilities increased. However, there was one particular engagement that, much to the amusement of several hundred school kids, Peter failed to keep. Jack Gallagher, then

Headmaster at Lisnasharragh High School explains: *"The evening of the School's Prize Awards is always fraught with difficulties but this one took an unexpected turn. The hall was packed with parents, shiny-faced kids, the Board of Governors, and special guests. We were waiting for the arrival of the Mayor to give out the prizes."* He smiles as he recalls how Iris turned up alone and quietly explained to him that Peter had been unavoidably delayed. *"It isn't often that a Headmaster has to explain to his amazed audience that their Mayor is unable to attend because he's been arrested! Still, I have to hand it to Iris. Under the circumstances, her presence showed a remarkable strength."* At the end of the evening the audience showed their appreciation with a standing ovation.

Since then Jack Gallagher and his wife Lily have become great friends of the Robinsons. In later years they met up while on holiday in America and enjoyed the easy familiarity that is the hallmark of all close friendships. Twenty years later the foursome would still be together for a special dinner to mark Lily's sixtieth birthday. Few would know the couple as well as Jack and Lily Gallagher.

Jack has this to say: *"I first met Peter through his membership of the Northern Ireland Sports Council. We got on well and his ability to listen and propose solutions impressed me greatly. In private he's relaxed with a great sense of humour. He's a bit of an expert on DIY as well as breeding Japanese fish! Iris, on the other hand, is definitely a people person. She loves to chat and is more spontaneous."*

There is no doubt that pupils took away more than a certificate of achievement from their prizegiving. They probably had a chuckle at the thought of their Mayor in police custody. But for Iris and her family, the situation was no laughing matter. Despite the British Government's insistence that, with the cooperation of the South, border security was watertight, Unionists were convinced that terrorists could cross it with ease.

Iris tells how Peter's presence at Clontibret had been a serious attempt to highlight the gaps in border security and that his role was simply one of observation. She adds: *"Originally it was Doc (Ian Paisley) who should have been there but he had to go to a funeral in America. Peter was asked to step in at the last minute. However, by crossing freely and unchallenged in such large numbers, they managed to prove that security was practically non-existent. Two hours later the police arrived and Peter was arrested. I was worried sick."*

Compared to her husband's predicament, the prizegiving may have seemed irrelevant, yet it was still a commitment. Kids and parents were expecting the Mayor of Castlereagh. As it was an important annual event for them, Iris believed she had to take Peter's place and make the best of it. *"I certainly hid my emotions behind a smile that evening!"*

While Iris fretted about her husband's brush with the law, Peter was beginning to wonder if he was in Ireland or taking part in an episode of the popular police drama, *Hill Street Blues*. If it weren't for the seriousness of his situation, the journey to prison almost sounds comical. Smiling, Peter recaptures the event: *"When the police arrived at the scene I didn't see any point in hurrying away. I was there to observe the event and had done nothing wrong. However, I was arrested and taken to Monaghan Garda Station where I was detained for five days before being released on bail."*

When he arrived in Dublin for the final trial, the court decided that instead of hotel accommodation Peter should go straight to jail. They soon found that their prisons while difficult to escape from were equally hard to enter! From Green Street Garda Station Peter was taken to Portlaoise Prison near Dundalk. *"What a journey!"* he laughs. *"A helicopter tracked us the whole way and the media carried live reports of the event."* By the time they reached Portlaoise, a prison that had some of the worst Republican terrorists of the time, Peter was amazed to hear he'd been refused entry.

He continues: *"The Governor explained that the prisoners had heard of my arrival and had started a protest riot. Apparently they didn't want me about the place. I was rushed back to the van as Garda officers radioed ahead to try and find me new accommodation."* Eventually the authorities decided that Limerick Prison was the best option. A new wing had just been completed and Peter Robinson became its first and only occupant at that time. He says with a smile: *"By the end of the day I felt I could write a hitch hikers guide to Irish prisons!"*

Despite Peter's slightly humorous note, he is well aware of the traumatic repercussions for his family. *"For Iris and the kids, it was a terrible experience. The fact that we lost all our security added an additional stress to an already bad situation."* Iris vividly recalls the evening they arrived home to find their security gates lying wide open and surveillance cameras gone. She tells of her anger and fear: *"After Peter was released on bail, pending trial, the Chief Constable of the RUC decided to remove our security. I was furious as well as terrified! Regardless of criminal accusations, Peter hadn't yet been brought to trial, never mind found guilty. There was no reason to remove our safety measures. We had young children and our details, including our address, were a constant source of media coverage. More than ever, the threat was real. We were left exposed and totally vulnerable."*

Peter will never forget an incident, concerning their middle son Gareth, that brought home to him just how much his children had absorbed. *"As often as possible, I tried to keep Saturday free. I wasn't very successful but that's beside the point. I attempted to prevent the garden from becoming a forest while Iris took the kids to Portadown to visit her mum. This was one trip that Gareth, then about six, loved. Suddenly we noticed that he was asking to stay behind with me."* It seemed strange but at first the couple thought nothing of the change in their child's behaviour. Then Iris finally discovered the reason. Peter continues: *"Apparently the lad was terrified that someone might come to kill me, and because of the noise of our ride-on lawn mower, I wouldn't be able to hear them arrive. He felt he had to stay and keep guard so that he could warn me. It's times like these that we got an insight into what our choices and lives have cost the children."*

After the loss of security the family received a lot of support from within the community. As soon as people realised that Peter was without protected transport, many offered their services. When businessmen clubbed together and bought them an armour plated car, they unwittingly provided a solution to more than Peter and Iris's problem. Purchased at auction, the car had once belonged to the Shah of Iran. With bulletproof glass as well as armour plating to body and chassis, not to mention a gas extraction system, it was undoubtedly a well-secured vehicle. Both Iris and Peter were overwhelmed by the generosity.

God's providential care did not end with the Northern Ireland politician and his family. He had a much wider arena in mind. As soon as their security was reinstated, Iris and Peter sold the car for a nominal sum to a missionary serving in a Third World country whose frequent encounters with bandits was making life increasingly dangerous. The car is still used on the mission field today.

One source in particular proved an unexpected but welcome aid for the Robinsons. Iris reveals how Eammon Malley's impartial political coverage on Downtown Radio was much appreciated. *"Eammon came to the house quite often to interview Peter and we got to know him fairly well. When we lost our security, he helped focus public as well as political attention on our plight."*

Iris laughs as she recalls the lengths that Mr Malley went to secure a special interview with the DUPs Deputy Leader. The fact that Mr Robinson was in police custody didn't deter him. *"When Peter was arrested, Eammon phoned the Garda Station and pretended to be Ian Paisley. It must have been a good impersonation – while Garda thought Peter was discussing circumstances with his Party Leader, he was actually giving a full account of the incident live on radio!"*

Regardless of what the public made of events, it was Iris and her children who had to deal with the consequences. Once Peter's trial got underway, Iris found herself catapulted into the glare of publicity. Day after day, as she left the courthouse, the frightened woman faced a barrage of missiles and insults. Angry faces pressed against the car window, hurling abuse and hatred. The media constantly dogged her steps hoping for a chink in the armour of Iris's loyalty to either her husband or their Party. Even an older, more experienced politician would have found the situation stressful.

Fortunately, Iris quickly discovered a novel and quite enjoyable way to cope. She chuckles as she recalls her method: *"It suddenly dawned on me that my wardrobe was of particular interest. For them, my taste in fashion was nothing more than a topic to attract feminine interest. For me, it became a façade for sheer nerves! A wardrobe of stylish outfits in bold colours was my way of declaring that the events would not wear me down. If they focused on my outward appearance, they left my internal panic alone!"*

After considering all the evidence, including forensic reports, it was decided that Peter was innocent of any charge against him. He was fined 15,500 Irish Punts and bound over to keep the peace for ten years. *"Despite what some opponents have suggested,"* he explains, *"I did not pay the fine. The authorities held on to the bail money. However, it was a relief when the trial eventually ended and I could get back to my family and on with my work."*

Iris too was relieved and, like her husband, is grateful to God for His care throughout such a harrowing time. *"The charges against Peter were ludicrous to begin with but it's frightening how things can spiral out of your control. Thankfully, God was over all. We had the best legal representatives who were able to gather all the necessary forensic evidence."* Of the eleven charges brought against Peter, only one was upheld. Technically, he was guilty of being present at an illegal gathering. It proved a difficult period in the couple's lives but it also provided an illustration of God's care and faithfulness.

Whatever else the Clontibret incident highlighted, it demonstrated Iris's ability to deal with media attention on a personal level. Over the years she had developed the skills necessary for public service and Peter's trial afforded the opportunity to put them into practice. With tactics of little more than smiling diplomatically and a sense of fashion, the fledging politician stepped from obscurity into the glare of publicity.

16

TAKING A STAND

LEAVING NORTHERN Ireland aside, there were two events that dominated the news in 1988. One, the collapse of the Berlin Wall, would go down in history as a symbol of liberty and an end to Communism in Europe. The other, a nuclear accident in the Russian town of Chernobyl, would become a living legacy of sickness and fear. For weeks, images of the horrific events eclipsed Belfast's usual servings of political wrangles and civil disturbance. As with all events of such monumental importance, the world may pause and shudder, but eventually life moves on.

Four years after the Clontibret incident, the Robinson's closed the decade with two birthday celebrations and an electoral victory! In between they'd also had their fair share of further ill health and stress, not to mention more prison sentences.

On one occasion, it was Iris as well as Peter who was behind bars. She frowns as she tries to find words to convey the depth of feeling behind the actions that resulted in her loss of liberty. *"It would be impossible to portray with any real accuracy my disappointment and anger over the Anglo Irish Agreement. I took part in every demonstration possible and was eventually charged with participating in a parade without giving seven days notice."*

Under the 'no taxation without representation' campaign Iris also refused to pay her car tax. Although aware of the possible consequences, she was prepared to go all the way to make her voice heard. In the end she was sent to prison. *"It wasn't a pleasant experience. I was alone for most of the time because other prisoners constantly made life difficult."* The worst part of the experience had nothing to do with prison monotony. It was simply that she missed her family. *"Rebekah was just starting school at the time and I really wanted to be there for her first day. As all mums know, that's a big milestone! In the end it was Peter who took her and both thoroughly enjoyed the experience!"* For Iris, going to prison was an extremely tough experience. It was equally stressful for her family but one she truly believed necessary and unavoidable.

Peter's view is equally pragmatic: *"At the end of the day, everyone wants the same outcome but not everyone is prepared to roll up their sleeves and get involved. They prefer to leave it to others. Iris has never been afraid to have the courage of her convictions."* As for any conflict between their actions and Christian belief, the answer is simple. Peter replies: *"If that had been the case, we wouldn't have acted as we did. It's as plain as that."*

Over the years, especially during the latter half of the Eighties, Iris demonstrated an aptitude and ability for the political arena. Her Party loyalties were clear as was her ability to interact with the community. One elderly constituent smilingly recalls: *"I've known Iris since she was a youngster. She was a real wee mother. When she grew up and got involved with politics, she didn't become like some. She still had the same down-to-earth nature. I'd go to her about any problem and know she'd do her utmost to help."*

When a vacancy arose on Castlereagh Council, Iris hesitated to put her name forward. She may have had the skill but as yet her confidence was embryonic and fragile. More importantly, she did not know God's mind on the matter. As usual when direction was needed, Iris prayed for guidance. *"When I received a word from the Psalms that assured me of victory, I submitted my name and then I told Peter! Naturally, he was well aware of my interest as we'd discussed the situation many times. Yet, as the deadline for submission drew closer, Peter wasn't at home and I had no means of contacting him. The mobile phone was still a long way off in those days! I knew he'd support me so I went ahead."*

She also told her friend Hazel Pickervance: *"Iris rang and said 'guess what I've done!' I couldn't believe she'd put her name forward for Council! Iris has always had a great way with people and there's no doubt she had the skill for the job, yet she didn't seem the typical politician. She's caring and compassionate but she was also very sensitive. However, as her friend, I supported her decision. It's amazing how far she's come."*

The person most aware of Iris's suitability for the political field was her husband. Iris recalls his initial concern: *"Peter and I often discussed the possibility that I might enter politics. Although very supportive he did express concern that my sensitivity might make me a little vulnerable to the cut and thrust of political life. However, he knew that I had prayed about the situation and hadn't done anything impulsively or lightly."* Peter adds: *"Canvassing door to door can be difficult. Iris is the type of person that if ninety-nine people give a positive reception and one slams the door in her face, she'll worry about the one that got away. She's a bit of a worrier by nature and I knew it could be hard for her."*

At one point it seemed that Iris had misread her divine guidance. Just as she put her name forward, the original Councillor changed his mind and decided to stand. Iris may have been mystified by the event but she was not dissuaded. Experience had taught her that God does not make mistakes. His direction was clear.

"When I learned that the other candidate had stepped back into the ring, I was a little confused. But my guidance was clear. There was no mistake and certainly there was no going back." Iris went to discuss the matter with her colleagues and after consideration it was decided that both candidates should stand. As things turned out, her colleague had second thoughts and decided to withdraw.

Apart from the political hiccup, another much more serious event threatened to thwart Iris's plans. When her mum was diagnosed with breast cancer, Iris's first reaction was to withdraw her candidature and look after her mother instead. *"For the first few days, like all families, we were in terrible shock. Politics was the last thing on my mind. I was ready to withdraw completely."* When her mum heard of her daughter's hesitation, she did some straight talking. *"Mum was determined that cancer should not get in the way of a normal life and insisted I go ahead with the election or she would feel responsible for the missed opportunity."*

Mrs Malloy's illness may have proved a challenge for her as well as the immediate family. However, it also provided Iris with a valuable insight into the difficulties faced by cancer sufferers. She realised the importance of sensitivity from the medical profession and quickly discovered the value of information and education.

Sadly, for Mrs Malloy and many women of the same generation, breast cancer was often a taboo subject. Many found the medical approach, at best, clinical and abrupt. When her mum was coldly and insensitively informed that the only option available was to 'whip it off', Iris was incensed. *"It's bad enough having to deal with cancer without putting up with such insensitivity. This particular doctor was known for his lack of compassion and bedside manner but there was no way he was going to treat my mum like that. I made an appointment to see him and insisted that before he 'whip' anything off, he do the appropriate tests to see if the cancer had spread."*

Iris and her mother needed to know all they could about her particular cancer and condition. Understanding the type of tumour and how far it had spread was essential information that would allow them to make an informed decision. As Iris left the doctor's office, nurses smiled and one even congratulated her for taking a stand.

When tests revealed that the cancer was localised and hadn't spread, Iris's mum agreed to a mastectomy. The early weeks and months following the operation were difficult for the whole family but especially for Mrs Malloy. *"Unlike today when women have a lot of emotional as well as practical support, my mum came home from hospital with nothing more than a few tissues to stuff in her bra. My heart broke for her. Physically and psychologically she was in terrible distress. The scars eventually healed but I don't think the emotional ones ever do."*

The experience was to leave its imprint on Iris. Politically, she endeavoured to do all in her power to champion the cause of women and the early detection of breast cancer. In later years she would advocate the importance of early screening and work tirelessly to raise public awareness.

Her mother's illness also carried a note of concern for Iris and her sister. The women, with a higher than normal genetic disposition, are acutely aware that they too may suffer the same fate. *"With mum's diagnosis, Marlene and I inherited a major concern for our own health. With a busy lifestyle it can be easy to allow things like mammograms to slide down the list of priorities. There are so many other things demanding our attention but sometimes the reality of the situation is brought forcibly home. I now make sure that mammograms are high on my agenda."*

Regardless of her personal circumstances, Iris still clung to the verse she believed God had given her. Twenty-four years had passed since her first teenage protest rallies and demonstration marches. During the intervening years as Peter's wife, she had experienced many of the harsher aspects of Northern Ireland politics. Lonely nights, media intrusion, and a lack of privacy were some of the aspects she wrestled with. She'd also known the fear of violence, been jostled and ridiculed by angry demonstrators, and even gone to prison for her convictions. The couple's children were also in the firing line when it came to negative attention or dislike for their parent's politics. Iris was well acquainted with the consequences of a political career, yet she firmly believed that this was the direction that God was leading.

For Iris Robinson, disobedience to divine guidance was not an option. So in 1989 she stepped into the very area where such incidents were the fabric of Northern Ireland's political life. God would take care of the problems that arose. With characteristic determination she launched herself into the challenge. She smiles as she recalls the busy weeks of electioneering that followed: *"Canvassing was hard work, something I've never been frightened of. I didn't mind the endless round of meetings and knocking on doors. Neither did heading off in the early hours to talk with nightshift workers bother me. Most people knew me and many had grown up with us. So, the social interaction was never a problem. It was, nevertheless, exhausting!"*

Her hard work paid handsome dividends. She earned the respect of constituents and eventually won a seat on the Council. She savours the moment: *"Success brings a brilliant sense of achievement. I knew I'd given it my best shot and was delighted with the result.   It was also a very humbling experience.   I had taken God at His word and proved Him faithful.   It was incredible to witness how God takes control. The glory had to go to Him."*

Despite all her efforts, her notable victory was tinged by a shadow of cynicism. Some suggested that it was her Robinson name, rather than any individual merit that had influenced voters. But, for Iris, there was no doubt in her mind that she had been called into public service. It would take, however, another twelve years of hard graft to prove her credentials.

17

POLITICAL LIFE

AT FIRST glance the 1990s promised progress and peace. The Cold War ended as the Soviet Union collapsed and Mikhail Gorbachev introduced his radical policies of 'Glasnost' and 'Perestroika'. The theme of freedom continued as South Africa celebrated the repeal of Apartheid. In Northern Ireland the instigation of talks and a declaration of an IRA ceasefire raised many hopes. But the horrors of wars in the Gulf, Russia, and Bosnia, as well as the appalling carnage of the Omagh bomb in County Tyrone, thoroughly shattered any illusion of human harmony.

For Iris Robinson the decade began with a sense of excitement and purpose. At forty life had suddenly changed direction and launched her into a fulltime career. After sixteen years of raising her family and running a home, Iris took on the challenge of local politics. Her new role at Castlereagh Borough

Council may have been the route toward an independent career but it also allowed her to support Peter in a more active manner. Using all the experiences and skills garnered from childhood and, perhaps, most of all, married life, she set about establishing her political identity as well as credibility. It may have taken several years but Councillor Iris Robinson would eventually emerge as a respected and reputable politician in her own right.

When she took her seat at the first session of Council, there was little sign of the confident DUP representative she would become. After twenty years of marriage to her Party's Deputy Leader, Iris was no stranger to the mechanics of official meetings. She was well aware of their format and procedures. Still, there was one aspect of political life that, like many newcomers, Iris dreaded. The very idea of speaking to a crowd of strangers could fill her with panic. Ironically, whilst Peter has no problem addressing huge audiences, his reserved nature doesn't relish the prospect of social chit-chat.

After years of working with young Party and Council members, Peter recognised the problem that many experience when confronted with public speaking and attempted to alleviate the newcomers' stress. His wife was amongst those who benefited. *"Peter told us we had to get used to the sound of our own voice. He asked us to begin by introducing ourselves and then proposing a hypothetical motion. It didn't have to be anything elaborate. The exercise was merely to help us get over the feelings of self-conscious awkwardness. I can still recall the tremor that rippled through my introductory speech!"*

Not everyone appreciated Peter's strategy. To some of the older members, unused to such apparent confidence, the young speakers were sometimes considered far too forward! For Iris and her colleagues, the exercise proved the best defence against tongue-tied embarrassment at public meetings. Although, she is the first to admit that it didn't always work! *"Even today I can be every bit as apprehensive! It's not easy when every pair of eyes in the room is fixed firmly on you. In those early days, I was often physically sick before a speech or meeting. Self-consciousness can be a really terrible problem that's hard to overcome."*

At such anxious moments, the nervous Councillor resorted to tried and trusted methods of coping: *"Regardless of how my stomach heaved or my knees knocked, nobody ever knew. I have always been able to hide my innermost feelings. When it comes to the public, makeup is my great camouflage. It's amazing how many women hide their vulnerability with a painted mask. With the makeup in place, I hold my head up, smile, and just get on with it!"*

Like most working mothers, Iris found it difficult to juggle the demands of a growing family and a developing career. In between Council meetings, she dealt with a variety of constituent's social and housing problems. The working hours were both long and erratic. People's worries or problems don't begin at nine o'clock and stop at five. Neither was it always possible for them to leave their home in order to seek advice or help.

The fact that Iris viewed her work as a 'calling' and not just a job ensured an extra dimension of dedication and commitment. In the early days of her career, the DUP Councillor made 'home visits' available to those constituents who needed help but, for whatever reason, were unable to leave their house.

Edel Patterson, a colleague from Castlereagh Council has built up a good working relationship with Iris. The two women have also become firm friends. Edel's regard for the busy politician spans many years of personal experience. *"I've worked with Iris a long time and know better than most how seriously she takes her work. She gives one hundred percent to every challenge but there's also a great sense of compassion and warmth for the individual."*

Edel has also witnessed Mr and Mrs Robinson's ability to work together. *"She and Peter make a dynamic team. They're both very professional and easy to work with. It's obvious that they're a family orientated couple. Peter is forever taking photographs, especially of the grandchildren. Their warmth and ease in each other's company is obvious and unmistakable."*

Edel readily admits that public perception is sometimes far from reality. *"There's no doubt that Peter and Iris have come in for their share of media criticism. It's unavoidable. Yet, in my experience, when it comes to people and their problems, the couple have always been fair and impartial, regardless of the individual's religious or cultural identity. The misconception that they favour their own community is rubbish."* Edel laughs as she adds: *"And, by the way, I'm speaking as someone from a different community!"*

Constituency service may have finished for the day but work is far from over. At home it is time to begin all over again. Laundry has to be sorted and the mathematical difficulties of children's homework solved. Unlike the problems encountered on a daily basis, the latter may be hypothetical but, at the end of a long day, they can be equally challenging! When it comes to domestic duties, parental fatigue is never an acceptable excuse. It's a balancing act that affects most working mothers regardless of the political divide.

Dolores Kelly, an SDLP Councillor and MLA, agrees: *"Regardless of how busy the working day, women are often faced with the additional demands of family and home. Women find that work just doesn't end at 5.30pm! I'm sure that most would agree that having a young family means being on call twenty-four hours. Iris and I may not share the same political views but our gender ensures we have a lot in common."*

DUP colleague Diane Dodds, also a wife and mother, finds politics a particularly demanding career especially for those with young children. *"As a mum with quite young children, I understand many of the difficulties Iris must have encountered in the early days of her career. Women may work in the public eye and in the community, but we still have to go home and cook dinner, wash dishes, and do all the other domestic necessities. It's far from easy!"*

The reward for such demanding occupations would fail to attract any but the most dedicated. Few would accept the currency of job satisfaction in lieu of financial restitution. However, according to Iris, those early days at Castlereagh Borough Council brought many things, although a salary wasn't one of them. *"In the beginning, the first year in particular,"* she explains, *"Peter subsidised all my expenses. He put petrol in my car and provided everything I needed. There was no payment whatsoever. It was possible to claim something like five or ten pounds for Council meetings that went beyond a certain time, but at first I didn't realise I could even have this basic allowance! By the time the Northern Ireland Forum materialised I got £200 per week and thought it was brilliant!"*

While Iris continued to forge ahead with what she saw as her particular 'calling', another Mrs Robinson was making her own political imprint. When the Republic of Ireland elected their first female President, Mary Robinson stepped on to the pages of history. Fifteen days later another chapter closed when Britain's Prime Minister Margaret Thatcher exited the world stage. Her successor, John Major, may not have broken the same barriers of gender, class, and education, but he was noted as Britain's youngest Prime Minister in over a century.

One of the disadvantages of life in politics is the lack of time available for the more private sphere. But in the early Nineties, the Robinsons suffered two family bereavements that brought them to a complete standstill. Iris's step-dad, Jimmy Malloy, finally lost his long battle with cancer. She did, however, take comfort in the knowledge that his eternal destination was certain.

"When I first met him he had no time for the gospel. Yet when he was diagnosed with cancer, the question of eternity loomed very near. When God brought the message of salvation home to him, Jimmy readily accepted it. When his cancer went into remission he continued to praise and worship God." Iris noticed the familiar symptoms and knew Jimmy's time was short. *"At the very end he simply said he was ready to go. I am thankful that when I get to Glory I will see not only my heavenly Father, but my dad and step-dad."*

Heaven's gates opened for a second time in 1991, when yet another member of the Robinson family was called home. On this occasion it was Peter's father who died. *"Peter's dad was a really lovely man. He was a very gentle and unassuming character with a real down-to-earth attitude. He left behind a wonderful Christian testimony but his death was a great loss to us all. Nonetheless, we had the consolation of knowing he too was with the Lord."*

The following year, 1992, the people of Belfast were served further helpings of mayhem and murder. As well as the devastation of grief that tore through the lives of individuals, an IRA bomb completely destroyed Belfast's forensic science laboratories. Many buildings, including houses and churches, in the close-by Belvoir estate were also badly damaged by the blast. Even Royalty appeared to suffer more than its fair share of tragedy. With three of her children's marriages in crisis, a major fire at her beloved Windsor Castle, and constant media intrusion, it was little wonder that Queen Elizabeth II described the year as an 'Annus Horribilis'.

Like most people across Britain, Iris was particularly saddened to learn that Charles and Diana had decided to separate. She understood some of the personal trauma the young Princess had suffered after the birth of Prince Harry and knew the feelings of insecurity that such depression brings.

In fact, for Iris, meeting the young Princess was one of the highlights of the decade. She recalls how as Peter's wife she was invited to accompany him to meet Princess Diana during one of her visits to Northern Ireland. Thrilled and excited by the prospect it was little wonder she took a long time deciding what to wear! In the end she settled for French chic and chose a navy satin outfit and a red hat. *"I've still got the gloves!"* she laughs. *"I have to say that Diana was incredibly beautiful and the media images just didn't do her justice. She was a few inches taller than me but the most striking thing about her was her lovely blue eyes. I found her charming and she put everyone at their ease. It was easy to understand why so many people loved her. She had a wonderful mixture of shy reserve and a great sense of fun."*

1992 also brought a few celebratory moments to the Robinson household. Peter was returned to Westminster at the General Election and Iris became Castlereagh Borough's first female Mayor. At first glance, a sensitive nature, knocking knees, and a dread of public speaking, are not conducive to a political career. But then, the task of raising a family would seem far beyond the skill or strength of a six-year-old child. Yet Iris proved more than capable on both counts.

Even today, she is certain that her ability to overcome weakness or vulnerability lies, not in any human strength, gifts, or intellect. Instead, her life has been at the centre of divine care and protection. She attributes the source of her success to God. *"It has been only through His power that I have overcome so many human frailties and weaknesses. It is He who can turn our insecurities to His glory. This is a lesson I learn every day of my life, God overcomes all things."*

18

NEW SEASONS

EVERY DECADE has its share of scandal, drama, murder, and tragedy. But the latter half of the Nineties served mega portions of each. In 1995 when Bill Clinton stepped off the plane and into Northern Ireland's media spotlight, there was no hint of the scandal to come. As the first serving American President to visit the Province, he and his family received a rapturous welcome. Yet, regardless of his many inspirational and encouraging words, there was one speech that completely upstaged him. When a nine-year-old girl revealed how her daddy's death at the hands of Loyalist gunmen interrupted her childhood with sorrow, she touched the nation's heart.

Peter Robinson, in his role as Deputy Leader of the DUP, was among those who received an official introduction to the President. It wasn't until eleven years later in 2006 that Iris finally met the American dignitaries on their home ground. The intervening decade had seen many changes on both sides of the Atlantic. Iris had been elected to both the Northern Ireland Assembly as well as Westminster but the curtain had fallen on Clinton's period in office.

Time may have moved on but, according to Iris, it hadn't left an obvious imprint on America's ex-First Lady. She smiles as she explains: *"I'd never met Hillary Clinton in person but media images led me to expect someone completely different. In reality, she looks younger than many of her earlier photographs. She's quite a tiny lady and, like many Americans, her teeth are perfectly straight and white! I've no idea if she works out but she's certainly very trim. Hillary Clinton appears an attractive and successful woman."*

In July 1995 yet another controversy was added to Northern Ireland's political melting pot. For the first time in almost 200 years, an Orange Order March was prevented from proceeding to the town of Portadown following its annual service at Drumcree Parish Church. The consequences were electric and trouble quickly spread across the Province.

Despite having no affiliation with the Orange Order, Peter and Iris Robinson were in total agreement with the protest stance that took place on Drumcree Hill. Peter was in no doubt where his loyalties lay: *"I've never been an Orangeman. In fact the 'twelfth' holiday provided a great opportunity to get the fish pond under way! However, I am a Democratic Unionist and not ashamed of either my culture or beliefs. I, like everyone else in my Party, stood foursquare behind the Portadown Orangemen for their stance."*

Two summers later, in 1997, a General Election brought yet another change of government when Tony Blair led his Labour colleagues into power. The media captured the smiles of triumph as the young Prime Minister and his wife greeted an enthusiastic crowd of well-wishers. In Iris's opinion, Mrs

Thatcher was still a hard act to follow. John Major may have been a friendly, approachable character whose interest in breeding Koi Carp fish provided a common interest with Peter, but he still lacked the charismatic presence of his predecessor.

The introduction of a Labour government also provided Northern Ireland with one of its most controversial and colourful characters. Marjorie Mowlam, better known as Mo, took up her duties as Northern Ireland Secretary and introduced her own brand of political protocol.

Whatever else was going on in the world, on 31 August there was only one event that occupied the news. The tragic death of Princess Diana sent shock waves around the globe. Iris has no problem recalling what she was doing when the news broke. *"I'd just come downstairs to make breakfast when I heard the announcement. I was completely stunned and just couldn't take it in."* With tears pouring down her face she raced upstairs to wake Peter. *"We came down and, like everybody else, sat in front of the television trying to absorb the reality of the tragedy. We sat there for ages, unable to leave the television as the events unfolded. Diana was so young and desperately in need of affection. I think she had very sad times with so many problems."*

Every year Iris has a constant and poignant reminder of the event. *"Princess Diana was buried on my birthday and I always think about her. I am continually reminded that there is no guarantee of tomorrow. Our life is in God's hands."*

On 6 April 1998 the media spotlight swung once again toward Northern Ireland's politics. This time it appeared that 'dialogue' had actually accomplished something. The world, as well as many in Northern Ireland, celebrated the signing of what became known as both 'The Good Friday Agreement' and 'The Belfast Agreement'.

The title may be a matter of taste but it was the actual Agreement that proved completely unpalatable to Iris Robinson and her Party. Her distaste for the situation is obvious. *"It seems incredible that criminals and murderers should be part of a democratic government. My Party's view is well documented and leaves no room for doubt as to where it stands on the issue."*

On a personal note, Iris admits to feeling 'shattered' by the event. *"It was worse than the Anglo Irish Agreement because it illustrated Government's complete unwillingness to listen. I think there was also a sense of helplessness in the Unionist community because our views were being ignored. Nevertheless, we determined to improve our votes and build the Party into a force to be reckoned with. History proves that has been the case."*

As the decade rolled on, it was Iris's private life that once again presented a new experience. Like many women, she was introduced to the new and unfamiliar role of mother-in-law! Unlike the proverbial stereotype, her relationship with daughter-in-law Angie got off to a promising start. Iris smiles as she goes on: *"Angie and I have a lot in common and share similar tastes. We've been known to go on separate shopping trips and bring back almost identical items."*

Iris's idea of a perfect daughter-in-law is simple. *"As parents we always want the best for our children. That's natural because they are our most precious commodity. But I'd decided long ago that as long as they love each other that's enough for me!"*

Angie tells about her first meeting with the Robinsons. Her future mother-in-law's flair for interior design made an impressive first impression. Iris's decision to give each of the rooms a particular theme is a talking point for many first-time visitors. But, on her initial visit, the hand-printed wallpaper and antique furnishings were completely lost on the young woman. *"I was far too nervous to notice the décor but I recall thinking it was a beautiful house. Iris has had a lot of fun choosing the*

Chinese, African, Italian, and Castle type themes. I think her favourite room is the 'castle' which is a rich tapestry of gold, blues, and deep reds." When Angie first met Jonathan, she had no idea that his parents were either politicians or in the public eye. *"I have to admit, I was a bit apprehensive when it came to meeting them."*

When Angie and Jonathan called at the home of her future in-laws, neither Iris nor Peter was home. As she and Jonathan waited, the young woman experienced a moment or two of panic! Angie laughs at the recollection: *"I was certainly more than a bit nervous. Meeting the in-laws can be a stressful situation! When I heard Iris and Peter arrive, anxiety got the better of me and at one point I remember fleeing to their bathroom to compose myself."* Angie needn't have worried. *"From the moment we were introduced, Iris chatted away, made me feel welcome, and accepted me immediately. We just clicked. Both she and Peter have always made me feel part of the family. They're also great fun on holiday, especially Peter who is forever popping up with his video camera!"*

As the couple's wedding day drew closer, Iris was almost as excited as the bride! With such a good excuse for a shopping spree, she lost no time choosing the perfect outfit. From her teens, Iris's outward appearance has always been important to her. Very often her public image is the best camouflage for private turmoil. Over the years she has developed a keen sense of fashion and knows instinctively what suits her best.

At the marriage of her son Jonathan, Iris's choice of an attractive pale blue two-piece suit was both stylish and understated. On this occasion, there were no media flashbulbs or controversial topics. Iris was dressed for only one role, the happy mother of the Groom. As with most that are given the same script in life, she ensured her mascara was thoroughly waterproof!

It should have been a wonderful day and, like all weddings, filled only with happy memories. However, at every future anniversary, the young couple would be reminded, not only of the sanctity of marriage but the sacrilege of evil.

Iris goes on: *"Jonathan and Angie decided to have a quiet wedding with just a few family and friends. Ironically, the date couldn't have attracted more notoriety. When my son and his bride took their vows and stepped into a new life together, it should have been filled with nothing but happiness; instead, every anniversary recalls the tragic devastation of the Omagh bomb."*

Peter was the first of the wedding party to learn about the horrific events unfolding in Omagh, yet he hid the knowledge from everyone including Iris, until after the reception. Angie tells how her father-in-law tried to protect them from the unfolding news: *"Peter must have been as shocked as everyone else but he hid his own feelings and tried to spare us for as long as possible. He showed great consideration and tact. Yet, once the news was out, it was impossible not to be affected."*

Iris, practical as ever, immediately took control and invited everyone back to her home for a cup of tea. By this stage, Peter was in and out for the rest of the day speaking with the media and keeping abreast of events. Despite the tragic circumstances, Iris and Peter did their best to ensure such a special day wasn't completely ruined.

Angie confirms: *"Despite everything we did have a lovely wedding."* Iris sighs as she comments: *"When Peter heard about the bomb he was completely devastated. It was impossible to prevent the horror from intruding for long. Many tears of sadness flowed that day. It's awful that Jonathan and Angie's anniversary has a link to such terrible memories. Perhaps it's also an opportunity to reflect on the sorrow of others as well as personal blessings."*

By the end of the decade Iris and Peter had celebrated yet another milestone in life. Almost thirty-three years earlier, the young Mr Robinson had watched mesmerised as his date's lack of appetite turned her Knickerbocker Glory into a liquefied mess. But as 1999 drew to a close, it was hearts, not ice cream, that melted.

Like all grandparents, both Iris and Peter revelled in the arrival of grandson Michael followed by his baby sister Olivia. Throughout their career Iris and Peter have welcomed a number of important guests at their home, yet the visit that raises excitement levels most is that of both Michael and Olivia. Granda Peter loves nothing more than his grandson's help in the garden or a 'huggle' from Olivia. Granny Iris has already introduced the young lady to the art of makeup.

Olivia's mum Angie laughs as she explains: *"Olivia heads straight for her Granny's makeup bag and Iris is always ready to lend a bit of advice. It's a hilarious spectacle when my daughter emerges from Granny's bathroom complete with lip stick and false eye-lashes!"*

Iris beams as she talks about those closest to her heart. *"Michael and Olivia make me feel so privileged and blessed. Peter and Michael are great mates and love nothing better than an afternoon looking after the fish or cutting the grass. Olivia has her Granda completely wrapped around her little finger! She climbs on to his knees for a 'huggle' and a chat and Peter is just chuffed."*

Peter's love and delight in the two young people is equally evident. *"When Jonathan and Angie's children arrive, they brighten the weekend! These two are special kids, and precious. Believe me, there's nothing more touching than a greeting from our grandson or a cuddle from our granddaughter. I watch Iris when they're around and it's amazing the effect they have on her. She simply lights up!"*

When asked about life married to a granny, there's an undeniable hint of pride in Peter's reply. *"It's hard for me to see her in the grandmother role. She looks far too young! There's not even a whisker in sight!"*

After a moment's reflection, Peter reveals another bonus from his latest and most important role. *"Childhood seems to be of a much shorter duration than ever before. Children grow up much quicker in our modern society. Yet, while it lasts, it is a wonderful time. I guess the treat for me is that in my grandchildren I find no guile. They have no personal or hidden agenda, no cunning, deceit or betrayal. All their words, actions, and emotions are honest, open, and real. I find that such a stark contrast with the world of politics. With my grandchildren, it's good to be able to drop my guard and simply be myself."*

As far as six-year-old Olivia is concerned, her Granda and Granny are the best. With pragmatic wisdom and perhaps a little of the Robinson genes, her reply is clear and succinct: *"My Granda is good and kind and I love him. I love hundreds of things about Granny too, and she's also a very pretty lady!"*

Teenage Michael adds his own thoughts: *"What can I say? They're just Granny and Granda. Granny is always there for me. What I really like about Granda is that he's always ready to talk. He knows a lot about things, not just politics. He listens to me and gives a serious reply. When it comes to computers or gadgets he's really up to date."* After a moment's reflection, Michael gives a further insight of interest to all kids! *"Granda and Granny are really generous with our pocket money!"*

Mum Angie knows better than most about their generous nature. *"When my niece in Australia lost her child and was then diagnosed with cancer, it was a double blow. Iris and Peter immediately rallied with support. With no hesitation, my father-in-law offered to pay my way to the other side of the world so that I could be with my family. It was an incredible offer of generosity and it is typical of the man. He doesn't wear his heart on his sleeve but his compassion runs deep."*

Perhaps it is Angie's next observation that reveals the true character of their Christian faith. *"The thing about Iris and Peter is that they are both genuine. When help is needed, they are there with sincere offers of practical as well as emotional support. That's what makes them different. Their kind of generosity isn't all hot air and words. It's the real thing. They live what they believe."*

19

HIGHS AND LOWS

TOM HANKS, in his role as Forest Gump, compared life to a box of chocolates. Sometimes it seems that someone has taken all the soft centres!

The allegory can seem equally appropriate in politics. As Iris quickly discovered, political decisions are sometimes hard and unpalatable. Her sterling work didn't always bring instant results. Sometimes it seemed that days as well as nights were taken up by endless telephone calls and paper chases. Yet, by the time the Millennium dawned, she had earned her fair share of recognition among constituents and colleagues alike.

She also knew what it was like to suffer the sting of criticism, something that Iris has never suffered lightly. Perhaps it's this aspect of life in the public eye that continues to prove the hardest to accept. Iris goes on: *"When newspapers print something unpleasant about me, I don't like it! That's a normal human response, nobody likes to read or hear unpleasant remarks. But, I accept that media attention is part and parcel of the job and I've grown used to the fishbowl type of lifestyle. I can even manage to ignore many of the unkind things people say!"*

However, when it comes to Peter or her family, it doesn't matter how many years have gone by, Iris's attitude is still fiercely protective. *"It has always made me furious to read something about Peter that is so blatantly untrue!"* Even worse are the slanderous or malicious stories that, over the years, have targeted them both. *"Peter in particular,"* Iris continues, *"has borne the brunt of some particularly vicious rumours in a bid to damage him politically. It hasn't worked. It never ceases to amaze me what imagination can conjure up. I've heard my husband accused of everything from infidelity, to domestic abuse, and even murder!"*

Such stories, regardless of how ludicrous or even laughable, continue to cause Iris concern, as she explains: *"Someone out there might just be daft enough to believe them."*

As with all who experience the distress that scandal inflicts, Iris reveals how she would relish the opportunity to expose the lies. Once again her passion against injustice comes to the fore. *"If only I had the evidence to take legal action! Unfortunately, the nature of scandal is that it's perpetrated by cowards and nobody is prepared to come forward to make their claim. They prefer to whisper in secret instead of being upfront and in public. This kind of dishonesty always makes me angry."*

No matter how much she detests rumours and innuendo, Iris is well aware that it goes with the territory. However, the experience has influenced her personal judgment. *"I hate gossip! When someone comes to me with a story about somebody else, my first reaction is to ask for proof. If it turns out to be mere rumour, woe betides the propagandist."*

Iris isn't the only one who shares the frustration of innuendo and media attention. Barbara McNarry, sister of the late George Best knows exactly what it's like. She explains: *"Nobody knows better than our family the distress that the media spotlight can bring. We've certainly got a long experience. I know exactly where Iris is coming from when she talks about seeing something unpleasant or untrue written about you or your family. There's an awful feeling of sheer helplessness and absolutely nothing we can do about it."*

After twelve years in political life, Iris knew exactly what to expect when she decided to run as the candidate for Strangford in the 2001 General Election. Despite failing in a previous attempt to secure the necessary votes, Iris believed that God had a further role for her in public service and refused to acknowledge defeat. *"If there's one lesson I've learned in life, it is that God doesn't make mistakes. I loved the work He had first given me in 1989 but I knew there was more for me to do. When the opportunity arose again in 2001, I had no doubt that this time God would open the door."*

Ironically, just as the campaign of 1989 had been threatened by domestic circumstances, Strangford also looked in jeopardy. Twelve years previously it had been her mum's illness that cast a shadow of doubt, this time it was her own. In fact, at one point, Iris was so ill that every waking moment was dominated by pain. Like many Christians, she discovered that the field of service is littered with obstacles. *"Whenever I look back at that particular time in my life, I am amazed at the outcome! It was only by God's grace and mercy that I even recovered my health, never mind win an election."*

The trouble stemmed from the same gynaecological problems that had haunted her married life. When surgeons left a little piece of ovary it was meant to help; eventually, though, it caused major problems and, in the end, it had to be removed. Like her nature, Iris's body is hypersensitive and, unfortunately, she suffered an allergic reaction to the anaesthetic. In the weeks following the operation she did her best to struggle on.

Wincing at the recollection she reveals the agony of the weeks leading up to the campaign: *"The pain was excruciating. I didn't know what was wrong but I kept telling myself it was just post-op problems that would eventually settle."* It didn't ease. The truth is it got so bad that Peter decided to call one of the doctors on emergency standby. Iris continues: *"The doctor arrived, took one look at me, and ordered an ambulance immediately."* Things went from bad to worse when at the hospital the doctor, unfamiliar with her case, didn't know what was causing the pain and prescribed exactly what the patient didn't need, another operation using the same anaesthetic!

The consequence was a complete nightmare. Even as she was wheeled out of theatre, Iris realised that the pain was no better. If anything, it had intensified. However, there is one blessing that Iris can link to those pain-filled days. She smiles as she remembers how, when at her lowest ebb, she opened her eyes to find Pastor James McConnell praying by her bedside.

The power of prayer is something that Iris has learned to value immensely. *"I know that nothing is impossible with God. No matter how bad circumstances may seem, and to me they have often appeared insurmountable, God can conquer all. At that particular time when I felt so ill, I couldn't see beyond my own immediate distress. Sometimes I wondered if I'd ever make a full recovery."*

Iris's body did recover from allergic shock and six weeks later she was, not only out of hospital, but back on the campaign trail. Her determination may have been as strong as ever, but physically she was still fragile from the after-effects of double surgery. *"Naturally, there were one or two occasions when I wondered whether I could continue. Surgery and illness had left me weak and exhausted. After twelve years in politics, I had established my credibility and had nothing to prove. Yet, I knew that God had not called me into retirement! There was still work to do."*

As soon as she felt a little more human, the DUP candidate set out to win the Strangford Constituency. It was a lot of hard work for everyone involved but there was also an element of good-natured fun. Iris laughs at one incident in particular: *"I seem to recall at one point we made a replica of a huge barge pole as a reminder of another party's promise not to touch the Agreement with such a nautical item!"*

Regardless of the humorous input, the DUPs campaign message evidently touched a chord with voters. By the time the count was finished, Iris Robinson was announced as the latest Member of Parliament representing the constituency of Strangford!

At fifty-two she, as well as two other successful female candidates, was on her way to Westminster. The pride and warmth in Peter's voice is unmistakable. *"Only I know what the campaign cost Iris physically. She had been very ill but she is a very determined woman! When we first set out in life together I never imagined where it would lead. I am very proud of her achievements. I have to say, I am very blessed to have her as my wife."*

Iris remembers the thrill of learning that the people of Strangford had chosen her as their parliamentary representative. *"I can't describe the emotion! People had listened, weighed up the arguments, and made their democratic choice. It was a very humbling experience to be chosen to represent them at Westminster. It was also a wonderful opportunity to give God the glory for the success."*

A special studio link allowed her to share the historic moment with her greatest supporter, Peter. With a beaming smile, she shares the memory: *"As the new MP for Strangford, I invited Peter to share a celebratory meal in my constituency! It was a very public moment but only I could read the pride in my husband's face. Peter is not by any means gushy or sentimental but he's an extremely warm and loving man. He*

*also appreciates hard work and effort and is never afraid to
offer congratulations and praise where and when it is due."*

Her first day at the Houses of Parliament was reminiscent
of the morning Iris arrived at Miss Greatrex's class in primary
school. Although a middle-aged grandmother, maturity did not
diminish any of her excitement as she entered the historic
buildings. With only three women among the eighteen
Northern Ireland MPs elected in 2001, it was little wonder that
she was so delighted. Even today, the event brings a huge smile
to Iris's face: *"It seemed like a dream! Imagine, a wee girl from
the Cregagh taking her place in the Mother of all Parliaments!
Westminster is an imposing and majestic place. It was an
incredible experience for me."*

As with all significant events in her life, Iris's thoughts
turned immediately to the 'gentle giant'. As she passed through
Westminster's doors, bitter-sweet memories of her dad flooded
her mind and brought a few tears to her eyes. *"My dad would
have burst with pride at the thought of his little girl taking her
seat in Parliament. Even his most imaginative stories could
never have come up with such a scenario! For him, as an
Englishman, my presence at Westminster would have been a
real honour."*

Of course, her election to Parliament was not Iris's first
introduction to the place. When Peter first became MP for East
Belfast, she had accompanied him to London. At that time she
had taken the opportunity to walk along streets that had once
been so familiar to her dad. Best of all was the chance to meet
with her Aunt Josie and cousin Norman. Once again, she picks
up the story: *"They contacted me and we arranged to meet for
lunch. It was so touching to learn that over the years my aunt
had followed Peter's career. But when I saw Norman, it was
like rushing back in time. He was my dad's complete double!"*

If Iris's lifestyle was busy prior to her election to
Westminster, it simply got busier! As well as car journeys, the

latest addition to the back benches was soon making use of trains, planes, and the odd taxi. Within a few months she'd settled into her parliamentary role and was enjoying the challenging, though hectic, pace of life. Although she may not have realised, her busy lifestyle was beginning to eat into the spiritual realm. With less time for prayer and fellowship with God, her storehouse of spiritual strength was fast depleting. Like many Christians in the same situation, Iris was totally unaware of the impending crisis.

Despite her growing reputation for hard work, it was still impossible to avoid the occasional missile of harsh accusation. When media reports suggested that Iris and Peter had their individual apartments in London, she was livid. These days Iris merely laughs at the absurdity. *"To set the record straight, no we don't have two apartments in London! MPs who live too far away to travel can claim an allowance toward the cost of remaining in London. Some use it for hotels or guest houses and some decide to buy a house and use it toward the interest on the mortgage."*

Iris goes on to explain that even in his early days at Westminster, Peter chose to come home whenever possible. However, when the need arose, the young MP, like his Party Leader, opted for more modest accommodation. Iris fills in the gaps: *"When Peter remained in London overnight, he stayed at the home of one of Doc's friends. By the time I joined him in Parliament there was no room for us both. I also had a lot more luggage to haul around and was soon fed-up with hotel accommodation. After a year, I'd had enough and we decided it was more economical to buy one apartment between us."*

However, there is still a spark of annoyance at any suggestion that MPs should not be entitled to their individual allowance simply because they are part of a couple. *"Somehow, I think there would be an awful lot of women complaining if they had to share their husband's financial allowances! TV or radio presenters who happen to be married wouldn't like to be classified as one item! Equality for women would take a big leap backwards if that was society's way of thinking!"*

Whatever Iris was or was not entitled to, there was one issue that was not up for negotiation. Despite the troubled and violent climate, she did not warrant any special security treatment. *"Peter was provided with a bodyguard but I had no protection whatsoever. I wasn't worried about myself, but my staff's safety was priority. When windows were broken and vandalised, I asked for a security camera. It was refused, so I decided it wasn't worth the hassle."* At the end of the day Iris decided there was only one thing to do. She installed the necessary grilles and a bulletproof door at her own expense. Her logic is simple: *"I didn't think it fair to expect people to take such risks for doing their job."*

Throughout her career, Iris has witnessed some of Northern Ireland's most historic events. Without question, her experiences will provide a rich tapestry of memories for old age. If the truth be told, there have been so many wonderful moments that Iris finds it practically impossible to choose one above another. She has met some lovely people including Prince Andrew who officiated at the opening of the Castlereagh Council offices.

According to Iris he was, as all princes should be, utterly charming! He chatted, joked, and waved at the lovely ladies in the building opposite. When his job was done, the only lady he wanted to take home was a beautiful figurine of a woman wearing a white hat. Iris quickly put him straight: *"I told him he had no chance! She was one of my favourite purchases when I had the opportunity to do what many women dream about – go shopping! I must admit, choosing the décor for the Council offices was one of my most enjoyable duties."*

As well as entertaining, there have been more than a few moments that have left a poignant tinge of nostalgia. Perhaps one of the most memorable was when the Council supported Peter's proposal to award the Royal Ulster Constabulary the 'Freedom of the Borough'.

Iris reflects: *"Despite encountering a lot of bureaucratic bigotry, the occasion turned into a wonderful tribute to the men and women of the RUC. People just appeared from everywhere to show their respect for the Force as well as appreciation for their service to Northern Ireland. I felt very privileged to have been part of such a touching and historic moment."*

20

MAKING A DIFFERENCE

TO MANY, Iris Robinson is simply the female voice of the DUP
at Parliament. Colleagues recognise her reputation for hard
work while constituents are drawn to her friendly, approachable
manner. However, when it comes to political ability, there is
one Strangford resident who considers the local DUP
representative at Westminster, a real asset to her Party.

Brought up in a home where Winston Churchill was both
friend and frequent visitor, it's little wonder that Lady Mairi
Bury of Mount Stewart House is so politically astute. When it
comes to politics, Lady Mairi has some very definite ideas. Her
opinion of Iris Robinson is equally clear: *"I was introduced to
Iris long before she became an MP. I liked her immediately
and found her straightforward attitude refreshing. By the time
she decided to stand as the representative for Strangford, I had*

no hesitation about signing her nomination papers. I believed she had the qualities and skill to make an excellent MP. I've had no reason to change my mind. She's a dynamic politician who gets things done."

A lifelong Unionist, the aristocratic voter changed allegiance to the DUP when political concessions appeared to weigh too heavily in Republican favour. Her voice conveys both frustration and annoyance at what she viewed as an intolerable situation. *"My family has a long history of traditional Unionist values. I became thoroughly fed-up when the Ulster Unionist Party began giving one concession after another. It was a terrible situation so I decided that the Democratic Unionist Party had been right all along and offered the better policy."*

Over the years both Iris and Peter have become very good friends with Lady Mairi. They are regular visitors to her Mount Stewart home and enjoy both the lively conversation as well as the delicious lunches. It's also obvious that Lady Mairi has formed a shrewd opinion of the DUPs Deputy Leader: *"I have developed a firm friendship with the Robinsons. They make a lovely couple. Iris is an extremely good-looking woman. Peter is just wonderful! I am very fond of him. He has a brilliant personality with a definite twinkle of fun. Like most people who know him, I find his sense of humour and wit completely charming."*

For Brenda and Norman McNarry, regard for the Robinsons had nothing to do with appreciation of either political skill or tactical manoeuvres. In fact, until 2006, the sister and brother-in-law of the late George Best barely knew the couple. Apart from a few polite words at his Freedom of the Borough Award ceremony and later his funeral, they had never met in any social setting. However, when they received an invitation to lunch at Westminster, the couple were extremely touched by the unexpected gesture of kindness.

"We'd always wanted to meet and personally thank the businessmen who made their private jet available to bring

George's body home to Belfast," Barbara explains. *"Iris and Peter had heard about this and invited us to have dinner with them as well as the people concerned. That was a really nice gesture."*

Barbara admits to a few moments of anxiety about the meeting: *"I didn't know either Peter or Iris and I was a bit nervous about meeting the Deputy Leader of the DUP. On television he appears so cool and aloof! I truly didn't expect to have the lovely evening that we had."* Husband Norman agrees: *"When we received the invitation, I never imagined it would prove such an enjoyable time. The Robinsons put us completely at ease. In private Peter is very different to his public image and I discovered he has a very witty side to his character. Iris is warm, down-to-earth, and passionate about her work. They certainly made entertaining hosts!"*

Regardless of what impression Iris Robinson makes in either political circles or individual's lives, few will hold her in as high esteem as Mrs Brenda Booth. In her opinion, the MP is nothing short of a Godsend.

Apart from the fact that they are both grandmothers, the two women have little in common. The parliamentary representative for Strangford hurtles through life at a hectic pace while seventy-year-old Brenda moves in a more sedate and easygoing manner. The event that would eventually bind them together occurred more than thirty years ago.

In 1969 as Iris busily prepared for her wedding day, Brenda, overwhelmed by grief, buried her five-year-old son. The future politician and the grieving mother knew nothing of the others existence.

When Iris first stepped out in faith into political life, she unwittingly became the instrument that would help Brenda Booth and her family find closure and peace. Brenda takes up her story: *"At just five years old, our son Lee had to undergo major heart surgery. Complications are always possible but we weren't expecting any problems. After nine hours of surgery we were told he was doing well and to go home and ring the hospital later. In those days parents weren't encouraged to stay with their child."* Brenda and husband Jack did as advised and left the hospital. It was the last time they saw their child alive.

"We rang the hospital only to be told that Lee had died an hour earlier. I can't begin to express the shock that completely overwhelmed us. We were numb with grief." Two days after they lost their son, Brenda's dad also died. The double blow caused immeasurable heartache. Eventually, for the sake of their family, the couple had to rebuild their lives and try to come to terms with the tragedy. Neither imagined that over thirty years later, they'd be living the nightmare all over again.

Brenda's ordeal began when she heard a news report alleging that Alder Hey Children's Hospital had retained the organs of children who had died in their care. As the scandal spread to include other hospitals, Brenda felt a twinge of fear and suspicion. Although her knowledge of Northern Ireland's hospital procedure was limited, the family desperately wanted reassurance that their little boy was not one of those affected.

"In those days I hadn't a clue about hospital practice regarding either organ donation or retention, but I did understand that teaching hospitals need body tissue. I also knew that I hadn't given permission to use any belonging to Lee. In fact, I didn't even know a post-mortem had been performed." Brenda wrote to the Belfast hospital concerned and got nowhere. It became an endless paper chase and the family's frustration grew.

"We decided to write to everyone we thought might be able to help us. We sent letters to all the MLAs explaining our situation. Sammy Wilson, whose father Pastor Sandy Wilson had buried Lee, did his best to get answers. Other local politicians like Mr Wells and Mr McCarthy also did their bit, yet there was no reply." Brenda and her family soon realised that, while local officials were only too willing to help, they

needed someone to raise the matter at a higher level. Having a voice at Westminster would add a little political clout.

Iris Robinson was used to fighting other people's battles. The only difference between the playground skirmishes of childhood and Brenda's case was that this time bureaucracy was the bully. But Iris now had the voice of maturity and the ear of Parliament to help her win the battle. The issues surrounding organ retention were complex and controversial for society as a whole but, for individual families, they were devastating.

As a politician, Iris understood Brenda's battle with bureaucracy but it was as a mother that she responded to her need. *"When I heard Brenda's story, my heart broke for her. What mother wouldn't be touched? The subject struck every nerve of emotion and for many it touched the very core of religious beliefs. I'd never be able to erase Brenda and Jack's burden but I decided to try and lighten the load."*

As the battle got under way, Brenda and Jack soon found that Iris's daughter Rebekah and son Jonathan had also climbed into the ring. *"We'll never forget the kindness and consideration shown by these two young people. Rebekah and Jonathan made sure we had all the latest relevant information. Jonathan told us about the Isaac Report and gave us useful online addresses. Their encouragement and support was invaluable as we encountered one obstacle after another."*

Before long Iris had inundated the hospital with requests for clarification regarding their practice of organ retention. She began asking questions in Parliament, demanding to know the exact numbers as well as the specific tissues involved. At one point, Brenda was told that administrative staff were unable to cope with the MPs demands. As time went on Iris became a voice, not just for the Booth family, but for hundreds of others across the country. Parents, unable to face the public spotlight, contacted Brenda to ask if Iris would speak on their behalf.

Brenda takes up the story: *"People from all sections of the community were affected. They were grief stricken and the last thing they wanted was publicity. At the same time, they too needed answers. I became a sort of helpline and Iris became their voice."* With dogged determination, she refused to take 'No' for an answer. It may have taken her years but the awful truth finally emerged.

Eventually Brenda and her family had to face the horrific news that Lee had indeed been among the children affected. *"I can't begin to describe my feelings when I learned that parts of Lee had been taken without our knowledge, never mind consent,"* Brenda sighs. *"Although we had suspected it all along, we weren't prepared for the shock. Nobody has any idea of the effect such news can have on individual families. I have seen people fall apart and marriages crumble under the strain. The knowledge that a beloved child's eyes, spinal cord, and other organs have been taken and used is an incredible burden."*

Even though it was impossible to cover the complexities of their experiences, Mr and Mrs Booth did find closure. More than thirty years after their son's death, in a private ceremony at the hospital, they donated the remaining sixteen pieces of Lee's body tissue for research into the death of children suffering from heart complaints.

As far as Brenda Booth is concerned, it wasn't only Iris's political input that brought them to the end of their journey, it was her compassion and genuine concern. *"I can never repay Iris Robinson for what she did. There were times when the sheer horror of the situation overwhelmed me but Iris kept telling me to stay in their face, refuse to back down, and eventually we'd come out on top. She's a real professional but it's her compassion and warmth that make her special."*

Brenda is surely one of Iris's most loyal supporters. But the respect and affection between the two women is mutual. *"It certainly was a long drawn-out battle,"* Iris admits, *"but the people who deserve the credit are Brenda Booth and her family. It took great courage, emotional stamina, and determination to unearth the truth about Lee. Brenda has an abundance of them all. I count it a privilege to have been able to help."*

In memory of Lee, and all the other children involved, a stained glass window was placed in Belfast's City Hall. *"As well as receiving an apology we were asked to contribute to the design of a beautiful stained glass window,"* Brenda explains. *"We decided to have a pathway leading to the tree of life. I think that says it all."*

However, the Booths hadn't heard the end of Iris Robinson for two years later they received an unexpected invitation. Brenda's delight and excitement is obvious. *"We couldn't believe our eyes! Iris had arranged for Jack and I to be guests at the Queen's garden party! We were over the moon and could barely wait! It turned out to be a really brilliant day."* Scarcely able to believe her eyes at the sight of so many famous people, Brenda watched as members of the Royal household moved and chatted with their assembled visitors. *"We'd never seen any of them before apart from on telly!"* Brenda laughs. *"It was a great experience. Afterwards Iris showed us round Westminster and we got to see all the historic rooms. Then we sat chatting, catching up on the latest news!"*

However, within half-an-hour Iris was off on another quest. This time it was finding a chair in the shade for an elderly lady. Brenda sums it up: *"There's nothing contrived about Iris. She's a born nurturer. Helping people is what seems to make her happy. It's also what she does best."*

21

LIFE GOES ON

THEODORE ROOSEVELT said that *"A great democracy must be progressive or it will cease to be a great democracy."* Northern Ireland's democratic condition may be open to interpretation but there is no doubt that by 2004 life in the Province had improved considerably. While terrorism and criminal activity continued, there was no longer the overt mayhem of the Seventies that had dominated every aspect of life. Belfast in particular was gaining a healthy reputation as a vibrant and attractive metropolis. The political climate had also experienced the winds of change and the Democratic Unionist Party was now the largest in the country.

No matter what President Roosevelt or any other great statesman had to offer, for Christians like Iris it is what God has to say that is most important. However, it isn't always easy to hear His voice above the clamour of everyday life. Neither does a busy agenda allow time for quiet reflection and prayer. Iris smiles as she explains: *"Every Christian knows the importance of time alone with God. It's essential to our spiritual welfare. Quiet reflective moments allow us to meditate on His Word and find nourishment for our soul. It's also when we bring all the troubles and cares that are wearing us down, leave them at His feet, and find peace."*

However, sometimes the business of life as well as service gets in the way. We become so occupied with the present that we forget the eternal. After the election in 2001 Iris's feet barely touched the ground. Running from one task to another and working three Saturdays out of four, there was little room for any personal life at all. *"I really enjoyed the work but I didn't realise just how much of my time was being eaten away. Neither did I appreciate how much it cost in the spiritual realm. Before I realised what was happening, I was skipping prayers or missing out on a daily Bible read. I began to make the mistake of relying on my own strength."*

With another election just around the corner, Iris's stamina and strength was fast running out. Physically, she was exhausted from the after-effects of yet another illness, this time a painful bladder condition. Emotionally, she'd plummeted to the depths of despair at the discovery of twenty lumps in her breast. Then, a few weeks later, she reached the peak of happiness to discover they were benign and not the cancer she feared. When her kitchen ceiling crashed to the floor, Iris thought she'd had her fair share of Christmas surprises. *"I couldn't believe how many incidents arrived at once. Some were merely frustrating and annoying but add them all together and everything seemed one huge insoluble problem. A General Election was about to get underway and, with all the additional stress, I didn't know which way to turn."*

With such a concoction of trouble, it was little wonder that stress levels were rocketing. As is usually the case, everything paled in comparison when Iris was confronted with news of a family tragedy. She recounts the horrific circumstances that finally pushed her to the end of her tether: *"Just as things seemed bad, they got even worse. Our family has always been close and shared each others joys as well as disappointments. When my young nephew introduced his girlfriend it was obviously a case of true love. Everyone was delighted and believed the childhood sweethearts would be together forever."*

As time went on, it looked as though the family prediction was correct. Everyone grew to love the young woman and accepted her as part of the family. No one could have imagined the sorrow that life had in store. With evident emotion, Iris continues: *"When we learned that the couple had been involved in a car accident, the shock was terrible. Although very badly injured, my nephew survived but the tragic incident claimed the life of his lovely young girlfriend. It was an awful time and the realisation that we cannot protect those we love certainly highlighted our helplessness."*

Yet, whatever the tragedy, life must go on. But returning to normal routine was something that Iris was beginning to find increasingly difficult. As she struggled to come to terms with her turmoil and confusion, an acute sense of powerlessness overwhelmed her. Suddenly the idea of being alone filled her with dread. Before she realised what was happening, Iris was not only in the middle of an election campaign, but a full-blown series of panic attacks.

"I'd never had a panic attack before and didn't know what it was. Suddenly, I felt vulnerable, afraid, and absolutely terrified of being alone. The sensation was really disorientating because it was so alien to me. After all, I was a seasoned traveller! I'd hopped on and off flights, travelled across the country, and stayed many nights in London by myself." Unable to make sense of the situation, it wasn't long before Iris was trapped in a vicious circle of fear. She cried constantly as she desperately tried to hold her crumbling world together. Peter, confused and distressed by her uncharacteristic behaviour, was at a complete loss as to what to do.

Most doctors agree that panic attacks are a common occurrence, particularly at times of acute stress. But only another sufferer can really appreciate the paralysing sensation of fear involved. There's often a tendency to underestimate the effect of panic attacks not only on the individual concerned but on the whole family. Lack of comprehension merely adds to the sufferer's distress making them feel even more isolated. Such attacks are never easy at any time, but as Iris found, a public audience made them worse. *"For me, being in the public spotlight at the time only aggravated the problem. The weight began to fall off me and I was aware that my gaunt and exhausted appearance was causing speculation. People couldn't fail to notice and would ask me what was wrong. I never knew how to reply."*

As the electioneering machine cranked up a gear and Iris grew worse, she was faced with a decision, as once again, illness overshadowed her career. *"During the 2004 election, I was completely distraught. Physically, I just didn't feel well enough to go on. It would have been so easy to step down and let it all go, I was so tired."* Worn out, ill, and desperate for guidance, Iris turned to God for comfort and direction. However, on this occasion she was faced with a new revelation that spoke loud and clear. *"It suddenly dawned on me that I hadn't been asking God's direction about anything lately. I'd been drifting aimlessly along, making my own decisions, and cramming my life with work. Even though I truly believed I was serving God, it was at the expense of fellowship with Him."*

Iris may have suffered many physical illnesses but at that moment she discovered she had a full-blown case of spiritual anaemia! *"Somehow I'd lost the eternal perspective. I'd been too busy for God. It can happen so easily. I don't think it's the big problems in life that make us lose sight of Him, sometimes it's just the small, ordinary things that distract our attention and, before we realise what's happening, we've lost the way."*

The Pastors at Whitewell had prayed many times for Iris's

physical welfare. When she needed spiritual guidance, they did not let her down. *"I could never thank Pastor McConnell enough. He as well as Pastors Sharon and Bertie were always there for me. However, in 2004, they reminded me that, no matter how neglectful I'd been, God hadn't left me. Regardless of our unfaithfulness He is waiting to welcome us back. I cannot describe the wonderful sense of peace that flooded my mind when these lovely Christians led me back to the Lord."*

Although the effects of ill health were still obvious, Iris had a new spring in her step as she set out to win the election. The panic attacks continued but were under control. She smiles as she explains her unusual therapy: *"Convinced that God had not changed my calling to help people, I got back into action. After all, the Bible tells us that we are to overcome the circumstances and press on to do His will. I may have felt like death warmed-up but, in actual fact, the routine of door to door electioneering acted as a sort of therapy!"*

It was the routine of work that proved most beneficial for Iris. Meeting and chatting to people provided a sense of order and normality to her day and the sense of panic subsided. Interestingly, this therapeutic practice stemmed not from any psychological self-help manual; Iris is certain that by simply obeying God and remaining in His service, she found the strength to overcome her fears.

It was at this point that God introduced yet another spiritual support to Iris's life. Her delight is apparent. *"When my sister-in-law Pat first accepted salvation, I was delighted! Yet I had no idea the impact she would eventually have on both my life as well as my service. Over the years I've watched this woman's faith go from strength to strength. It is amazing to see how God has used her."*

Today, Pat serves and ministers at Light and Life, a Free Methodist Church based at Dundonald. Neither woman imagined the role God had in store for them. For Iris, her sister-in-law has become a powerful instrument of spiritual ministry. *"I have learned more at this little church, especially under my sister-in-law's teaching than I ever thought possible. Pat is determined to bring the gospel to the whole community and I count it a privilege to be able to play some small part."*

It was Pat, together with other women from her church, who helped comfort Iris throughout her crisis of panic. Since then they have become some of her closest friends. Eileen, who sings with Iris during praise and worship, tells of their close bond of friendship: *"We may come from very different communities, but as Christians, Iris and I are as close as sisters. I've witnessed an amazing transformation in her life. She came through an immense trial but has emerged a new woman of God. It's difficult to sum her up in just a few words but it really is a joy to know her."*

Carol, another friend and member of Light and Life who counts Iris as family, has this to say: *"I'd only known Iris Robinson in her role as MP. However, since she came to our church, I've seen the real woman! She may move in different social circles but there's no airs or graces. She's down-to-earth and loves nothing more than to kick her shoes off, put the kettle on, and enjoy a sisterly chat."* After a moment's reflection, Carol sums up their friendship: *"To put it simply, I like her company because it's obvious she's a woman who personally knows the Lord."*

Illness may have cost Iris, and those closest to her, a lot of concern and distress, but when it came to commitment and service, she took Scripture's advice. Iris pressed on, stayed in her 'calling' and, not only secured her Westminster seat for a second time, but found an unexpected source of blessing. Iris has discovered, not only an added dimension of Christian fellowship, but love and acceptance from those who belong to yet another branch of the family of God.

22

SIMPLY THE BEST

IT DOESN'T really matter how 2005 began, for the citizens of Northern Ireland the events of 25 November brought the year to a tragic and unforgettable close. With an estimated crowd of over 100,000 the funeral of George Best was among the largest the country has ever seen. Despite driving rain and biting icy winds, people came from everywhere to say farewell to the man who, in his lifetime, had become a football legend. Appreciation for his talent and skill had never been the monopoly of one community. Neither was the sorrow at his passing.

Both Iris and Peter followed the career of the 'Belfast Boy' whose playground had been the working-class streets of Cregagh. In 2002 Castlereagh Borough Council unanimously accepted the SDLPs proposal, which Peter seconded, and awarded George Best the Freedom of the Borough in recognition of his contribution to football. *"It turned out to be a fantastic day for all of us and we tried to make sure it was equally special for George."* Iris smiles: *"Credit has to go to Edel Patterson and Joan McCoy who worked tirelessly to make sure everything went smoothly."*

George may have enjoyed the lunch at La Mon House Hotel but, as he later revealed, the award ceremony at the Council offices was one of the most nerve-wracking experiences of his life! The unexpected appearance of some of his closest friends added an extra special note to the day; the look on George's face made all the hard work worthwhile. When he saw Denis Law and other celebrity guests he was stunned; his delight was obvious.

Perhaps the most touching aspect of the day occurred at the Best family home when George unveiled a commemorative plaque and reminisced about his boyhood in the Cregagh estate, where Catholic and Protestant neighbours had lived side by side. His lifelong non-sectarian attitude raised him above the religious divide and ensured support from both communities. The football hero had a fantastic time but, as the day progressed, it was apparent that he was completely exhausted. *"It was obvious that George was tiring,"* Iris reflects. *"Yet, regardless of how he was feeling, he continued to meet everyone who had waited to speak to him."*

Despite his evident illness and frailty nothing prepared the people for the news of George's death. Just three years after the award ceremony, he passed away in the intensive care unit of London's Cromwell Hospital.

When it came to the funeral arrangements, few of George's relatives could have envisaged the scale of the event. To the world of football, George may have been a sporting legend but to those closest to him, he was simply family. Shortly before he died, his sister and brother-in-law, Barbara and Norman McNarry, bumped into Adrian Donaldson, Chief Executive of Castlereagh Borough Council. Norman explains: *"We were at the airport on our way to visit George and I think Adrian managed, from the poor prognosis, to gauge the seriousness of the situation and was prepared for the outcome. However, I don't think any of us could have foreseen the magnitude of the event."*

Edel Patterson may have enjoyed her role in organising George's Freedom of the Borough Award, but when she received a phone call from Norman asking if the Council offices could be used as a venue for his brother-in-law's funeral, it was truly one of her saddest tasks. Fortunately, the call coincided with the Council's monthly meeting and Edel was able to contact the Chief Executive immediately and asked him to raise the matter. It was soon apparent that such vast numbers, not to mention the issue of security, rendered the Council offices completely inadequate.

Another venue had to be found. Iris takes up the story: *"Peter rang the Secretary of State to ask if Stormont could offer a better alternative. To his credit, Peter Hain had no hesitation and even made funds available."* The actual event, as most of the world has witnessed, was incredible. Outside, flowers carpeted the steps of Stormont. Inside, the atmosphere was deeply emotional as people offered their tributes and memories to the much-loved George Best.

But whatever kind words, anecdotes, or tributes for George, there was only one piece of news that, for Iris, would have brought a glimmer of hope. *"The funeral service was beautiful. Everyone had their own fond stories about George and the atmosphere was emotionally charged. I found it impossible to hold back the tears. To know that George had made peace with God would have made the event so much more bearable."*

Like all who share her faith, when confronted by the finality of death, the question of salvation was uppermost in Iris's mind. Aware that George's sister Carol was also a Christian, Iris took the opportunity to speak to her after the funeral. In a quiet corner of La Mon House Hotel, Carol shared the news of her brother's salvation.

The delight in Carol's voice is unmistakable: *"I may not know Iris very well but as Christians we both appreciate the value of God's salvation. It is something we all want for our families. After the funeral, at the hotel, Iris came over to speak to me and I was able to tell her that George had not only heard God's Word but had believed it. Three weeks before he died, George truly accepted Christ as his Saviour. I had no doubt then and have none now. I know with a certainty that my brother is in heaven."*

The memory immediately brings a huge smile to Iris's face. *"What a testimony of hope to leave behind! When Carol told me that George had been saved, I was really overjoyed. As all Christians know, death certainly brings much heartache but the knowledge of salvation gives wonderful comfort."*

When she met one of the professionals who had looked after George Best, Iris was once again reminded of God's compassion. *"I had the opportunity to speak with one of the doctors who cared for George in hospital. He is a lovely, gentle man of God. He told me that George's nurse, also a Christian, read the Scriptures to her famous patient every day. How wonderful that the final weeks of George's life were filled with the news that God loved him."*

George Best was blessed to have such caring professionals at the end of his life. Not only were they expertly attuned to his physical needs, but fully equipped to tend to his spiritual welfare. Yet, it wasn't the first time George had heard the gospel. The seeds had been sown many years before when, as a youngster, he attended both Sunday school and children's meetings at Mount Merrion Free Presbyterian Church.

Iris also recalls the summer evenings when children from their neighbourhood flocked to sit on the grassy verge and listen to the message of God's love. With rapt attention they listened to many wonderful stories about Jesus. *"Although I didn't go to the actual church, the open air services for kids were great. I used to sit with the others and hear exciting tales of biblical characters like David and Goliath!"* No doubt, George also enjoyed the same heroic narratives. More importantly, he absorbed the simple news that Jesus loved him. It was a fact that the youngster never forgot. In later years George would tell how the lessons of childhood instilled a respect for the things of God.

It may have taken a lifetime between sowing and harvesting, but as George's testimony proves, the seed of God's Word is never sown in vain.

23

WHERE TO NOW?

SHE HAS come a long way since the teenage days of protest marches, demonstrations, and political rallies. Time and maturity have tempered the idealistic dream and curbed the youthful impatience for change. But, almost four decades later, Iris Robinson's passion has not altered, neither has her Party affiliation. She continues in the unshaken belief that the Democratic Unionist Party holds the best political recipe for lasting peace. The fact that it has grown to be the largest Party confirms and justifies such allegiance.

"Time moves so quickly! Sometimes I find it incredible that between us Peter and I have notched up almost eighty years experience with the DUP." The colourful rallies and passionate speeches may have whetted the teenager's appetite for political life, but it was marriage to Peter that showed her the

commitment it required. *"After we married, Peter threw his lot in with Doc and concentrated his skills on building the Party. Today people see the end product but they have no idea what it cost. Believe me, it was a long hard slog."*

The most precious investment for the Robinson, as well as the Paisley household, has been that of time. *"Like Peter, Ian had to sacrifice a lot of his home life. In the early days they toured the country trying to motivate and encourage people to join the DUP at all its various levels. I'm sure that like myself, Ian's wife Eileen, knew a lot of lonely evenings."*

With time as the currency, there was little to squander on socialising. Any free moments were hoarded to spend a little extra on family life. Yet Iris soon found that even this meagre allowance was not sacrosanct. *"It wasn't unusual for me to come downstairs in the early hours of the morning and find Peter still working on our manifestos or other political papers. Of course, in later years, as the Party grew and expanded there were others to help; whereas, in the beginning, everything had to be done from scratch. Peter isn't the sort to jump in front of cameras. He believes in what he's doing so he simply gets on with it."*

Today, with the foundations well and truly laid, the DUP is experiencing a huge measure of success. When it comes to their future, Iris once again turns to her Christian faith. *"Well, it's hard to predict the political future of the Province. But there's one thing I know for sure! God hasn't brought us this far to let us down now. I'm certain that the Party's political position is fundamentally sound. After more than thirty years in politics, I've witnessed many changes but I still believe that government can only belong to democrats. Until Republicans have permanently ended all terrorist and mafia-style activity, they won't meet the basic criteria for inclusion. It's as simple as that."*

When asked how her Party can be certain that any cessation of such activity is permanent, Iris sighs before going on: *"I don't think we could ever be absolutely certain. Over the years I've seen too many of their broken promises. So, yes, there could be a danger that Republicans could regress even if we reached a stage where an Executive was in place. We would need to have safeguards ready to protect democracy as well as the Unionist position and ensure a heavy penalty for relapse."*

Although Iris cannot be drawn on specific plans regarding an Executive, she is certain that it won't conform to any previous political norms. *"There just wouldn't be sufficient trust. Eventually, it could become a constant round of apprehension and suspicion, albeit, in a political setting. Yet, like every other sane person in the country, I too welcome the opportunities for economic prosperity and social improvements. Nevertheless, there's no point in glossing over major problems. If the foundation isn't right, any future progress would prove shaky and ultimately collapse."*

Whatever changes the future holds for the DUP, Iris Robinson is determined to alter its shape. *"We need to see more women in political life but, primarily, we want more in the DUP! I'm determined to do my bit to ensure that our Party benefits from the unique talent and skills of the female gender. Already Baroness Paisley has sounded a female voice for us in the House of Lords. What an incredible opportunity for women!"*

Her enthusiasm for the subject is obvious and her plans to attract more women have already begun with a recruitment drive in London. *"For a long time I'd hoped to organise a seminar for women in Northern Ireland. I believe that there's a lot of young talent out there that just needs to be encouraged toward a political career. Eventually, thanks to the efforts of Margaret McKee, the DUPs parliamentary secretary, we held the prototype in London!"* With female speakers, a tour of Westminster, and an opportunity to ask questions, the event proved a huge success and the Strangford MP is eager for a repetition on her home ground.

"I can't wait to have a similar event in the Province. The one in London was fantastic as well as a lot of fun. The former Speaker of the House of Commons, Betty Boothroyd, called in and added a touch of her unique brand of wit and sparkle. She's a fantastic woman and a great character who has promised to lend her support. I think she's a wonderful role model."

When asked how she sees her own role in the future of Northern Ireland politics, Iris shrugs as she replies: *"I'll be there for as long as my constituents want me to be there. However, my destiny is ultimately in the hands of God. Nobody can alter what He has in store for me. Basically, my role in politics will last until He decides otherwise."*

Whatever the future holds for Iris politically, it would seem that another field of Christian service has already opened. Although hesitant to emphasise her input, Iris is passionate about what has become known as 'prayer hampers' for the local Free Methodist Light and Life Church. *"Some members of the church came up with the idea of revealing God's love to the community in a very practical manner. It sounded great and after a lot of prayer we decided to go ahead. It is amazing how God has blessed the work!"*

What began with just a few tins of food has turned into thousands of pounds worth of goods. Now, instead of a garage shelf, what's known as 'heaven's storeroom' has expanded to almost warehouse dimensions. Recipients of a 'prayer hamper' are usually selected on a referral basis and the church then tries to meet the individual's specific needs. Iris explains how donations of everything from toothpaste to tea bags are meted out to those in most want. *"We can supply everything from fresh meat and vegetables to a kitchen table and chairs. It's an attempt to reach out and try to give someone a helping hand enabling them to get back on track and overcome hard times. That's the kind of love I believe Jesus wants from us – to get up and do something!"*

Another source of spiritual nourishment is the women's Bible study held at the home of her sister-in-law Pat. Inspired by the fellowship and warmth of such an informal setting, Iris is keen to open her own doors as an alternative venue. *"I'd love to have a women's study group in my own home and it's something that, God willing, I plan for the future."*

There's no doubt that the local church plays a prominent role in Iris's Christian service. In the summer of 2006 they invited her to join their worship team at the *Rachel's Well* seminar for women, but few realised how much the opportunity really meant. *"When I was asked to sing at the event, I was stunned! Throughout my Christian life it has been my dream to be part of a musical ministry. I simply love to praise the Lord in song. The seminar turned out to be a wonderful day with a real sense of blessing. I poured my heart into every song. In fact, for the next few days, I was hoarse!"*

Apart from a 'powerful' ministry at the Free Methodist Church, Iris is also attracted by the friendly, intimate atmosphere. She has formed many friendships among the women who attend. *"The women I have met have incredible testimonies. It is easy to see the power of God at work in their lives. One young woman in particular, Margaret, is an inspiration to us all."* Iris goes on to reveal how, despite the medical expert's poor prognosis at her daughter's birth, Margaret's mother Edith knew that God could work wonders for her child. *"Today this young lady writes poems of praise and thanks to God. To me, she's a real trophy of grace."*

As a couple, Peter and Iris continue to worship at Whitewell Metropolitan Tabernacle. Pastor McConnell's brand of scratching-where-people-itch ministry, plus an inspirational choir, make the church a firm favourite for both Robinsons. *"Peter and I love Whitewell. We've known Pastor McConnell for many years and admire the dedication he gives to his work. On a personal level, his prayers and consideration for me and my family have been much appreciated."*

As well as ministry and song, the busy politicians are always guaranteed a seat! With a smile, Iris reveals her secret: *"Sometimes flights are delayed and I can end up running late, that's when I can depend on my wee mates to keep us a seat! I've many friends at Whitewell but I really have to mention Betty, Jean, Isabelle, May, Robina, and a lovely couple named Harry and Maureen. They know me particularly well, plus they're responsible for keeping the seat!"*

There's no doubt that for a woman from her generation and class, Iris has achieved a huge measure of success in her career. At fifty-seven she has been cast in a few of life's most interesting and exciting roles. Yet the one she loves most has often proved the most painful. Like many women, Iris's family is her strength as well as her weakness. Her sigh is recognisable by all mothers who every now and then climb aboard for the inevitable guilt trip. *"There's no instruction manual for motherhood. We can only do what we think is best and sometimes we get it wrong. Apart from saying sorry, there's nothing more we can do."*

Her regret of not spending enough time with her children is a common complaint of all working mums. However, as she points out: *"When I see how our three turned out, I have to confess to a glow of maternal pride. They're all lovely individuals. We must have done something right!"*

Iris is the first to acknowledge that a high profile career placed enormous stress on young shoulders. *"I believe God has protected our children and they are stronger people. I have been terrified by the knowledge that my daughter carried a bomb from her dad's office, yet I was amazed by her courage. The same scenario was repeated with our sons, and they too showed immense strength of character. How can I not feel such pride?"*

Parental interest and concern does not end with a child's maturity. The sorrow of a son or daughter is equally acute for their parents. When daughter-in-law Vicky was diagnosed with cancer, both Iris and Peter shared the devastation and shock.

Although a painful experience, the incident provided Iris with an opportunity for a personal encounter with God. *"Gareth's wife Vicky and I have always been great friends. I really have been blessed with lovely daughters-in-law. As Christians we have an added dimension to our relationship. When she was diagnosed with cancer, we couldn't take it in. It didn't seem possible, she appeared so young and healthy."*

Despite everyone's prayers and words of encouragement, Iris was desperate for a personal sense of God's assurance. She wanted Him to tell her that Vicky would be okay. *"Finally, I closed my sitting room door, knelt on the floor, and brought Vicky before the Lord in prayer. I was determined not to leave the room until I knew without doubt that my daughter-in-law would be healed. By the early hours I opened my Bible and read the answer in John 11:4. The news that 'this sickness is not unto death' calmed all my fears!"*

After that, Iris never doubted that Vicky would recover. It was a long hard journey for the young woman and, similarly, she has her own personal memories of drawing close to God. Before long the whole family shared Vicky's thanks and joy when God honoured His promise and she received the all-clear.

As a middle-aged woman, Iris has few of the more obvious signs of ageing. Blessed with clear skin and a slim figure, she retains a fresh and youthful appearance. She laughs when asked for a few beauty tips: *"It's impossible to hold back time. After fifty everything definitely migrates south and it isn't coming back! Like many women I do what I can with what's left. I colour my hair, choose styles that suit me, and use makeup to full advantage!"*

Apart from the cosmetics, Iris has discovered an enjoyable way to ensure her heart stays healthy and her dress size remains a ten. An extra bonus is that Peter shares his wife's enthusiasm. *"We've taken up cycling! Now, instead of the London Underground, we take our bikes. It's a great way to build up stamina and it keeps the weight down. I noticed Peter getting a bit too cuddly,"* Iris jokes, *"so I thought we could burn up some calories and enjoy being a twosome again!"* Whether or not the DUP Deputy Leader and his fashionable wife will fall victim to the cyclist's fluorescent Lycra is anyone's guess. According to Iris, it isn't on the agenda!

She may be middle-aged but there's no sign of her slowing down. In fact, as a politician, her work schedule is busier than ever. Within the church, her service is branching out in new and exciting directions. Yet Iris has never been happier or less stressed. *"My life still has problems. Things still cause me confusion and pain but that's how it is for everyone. Christians aren't exempt from trouble. For me, a few moments before God give me the strength and comfort I need to face each day. To keep our eyes on the Lord and keep going is the best any of us can do."*

Like many Christians, Iris has proved that such reliance upon God is the best policy of all. She identifies fully with Paul's aspiration in Philippians 3:14, where he writes: *'I press on toward the goal to win the prize for which God has called me.'*

POSTSCRIPT

"*For me, this biography has been a real journey of discovery. I have laughed at some of the memories Lorraine has unearthed and cried at much of the remembered hurt. I've also been amazed by the sheer magnitude of God's provision and mercy. Hindsight has given me a wonderful view of divine sustenance and care. It is a rich blessing to experience unconditional love at any season of life. My dad and then my husband ensured me a lifetime's supply. I may not be able to thank my 'gentle giant' this side of eternity but, for all that he has done, I'd like to give Peter his portion today.*"

Iris Robinson